Bill Hosokawa

OLD MAN THUNDER
FATHER OF THE BULLET TRAIN

SOGO WAY

DENVER, COLORADO

Published by Sogo Way, 1099 18th Street, Suite 2020
Denver, Colorado 80202 USA

ISBN 0-9659580-0-0

Library of Congress Catalog Card Number: 97-69044

Manufactured in the United States of America
First Edition

Also available as an audio book

Dust jacket design by Doris O'Brien and Nicole Trousdale
Maps by Kim Long, © 1997 Sogo Way
Book design by Marilyn Auer
This book is composed in Goudy Oldstyle and Dragon Extra Bold
Printed by R.R. Donnelley & Sons Company
The design on chapter pages is based on calligraphy by Shinji Sogo.
It is his motto: "Nothing is impossible."

Dedicated to the thousands of men

(and a very few women in the

then-male-dominated Japan)

whose faith and talents enabled

Old Man Thunder to realize

his dream of creating the

marvelously beautiful Bullet Train.

TABLE OF CONTENTS

Note: Photographs follow pages 80 and 144

NOTE: Throughout *Old Man Thunder*, the spellings of Chinese cities, geographical locations, and names are in the romanization system called *pinyin*, introduced by the Chinese in the 1950s. This system replaced the Wade-Giles system and the place-name spellings of the *Postal Atlas of China*. Please see *Glossary and Terms* on page 220.

INTRODUCTION

Shinji Sogo was a Japanese bureaucrat who, to borrow a word from another culture, had the chutzpah of a robber baron in the golden days of American entrepreneurship. This is not to say he sought power or wealth. He lived modestly and scorned the trappings that came with prestige in the developing Japan before and after World War II.

He had chutzpah in the sense that, in pursuit of what he believed was best for his country, he flaunted convention in a land where and a time when conformity was the only accepted mode for respect and success. Nurtured in a society built on reverence for precedent, protocol, and for strict adherence to rules, he rose through the ranks of government bureaucracy. Yet there were early hints of underlying rebellion and independence. In the final years of service to his country, he dared to mislead tradition-bound superiors, without zealotry, because he was convinced that what they were about to do was a mistake.

Sogo dared to commit his nation to the massive, revolutionary Bullet Train project—comparable in terms of boldness and national significance, although certainly not in technical achievement, to the American program to land men on the Moon. He made the commitment knowing full well that the budget estimates he submitted were only half of what the true cost would be. He knew that the very size of a more realistic estimate would give the many powerful opponents of the project more arguments for blocking it. Worse, they would lead the National Railways on an ultimately more expensive, makeshift course that would only delay solution of the nation's paralyzing transportation problem. So, regardless of personal consequences, he dared to commit his nation—with deceit, if you will—to a vast transportation project that turned out to be the indispensable underpinning of Japan's spectacular economic growth. It is hard to imagine Japan today without the Bullet Train system that stitches its cities together with a swift, safe, incredibly reliable mode of transportation.

I first heard of Shinji Sogo in 1964 when, on a trip to Japan, *Reader's Digest* magazine commissioned me to look into the then developing Bullet Train as a possible story. The *Digest* was interested in an article focusing on the marvelously exciting train itself. The obstacles leading up to its creation were a lesser part of the story. In my research Sogo's name came up as president of Japanese National Railways (JNR) and father of the project, but I did not meet him. My story, incidentally, was published in April 1965.

Shinji Sogo's youngest son, Shinsaku Sogo, at the time was

stationed in the New York office of JETRO (Japan External Trade Organization), a semi-government agency whose mission is to promote business between Japan and the rest of the world. The younger Sogo wrote to thank me for the story, and we kept up desultory contact over the years. He went on to become managing director of JETRO's worldwide network. In 1990 he retired, and he and his wife, Machiko, moved to Denver, Colorado, where I live.

Shinsaku and Machiko planned to spend the rest of their years working for better understanding between Japanese and Americans. Their vehicle was a modest nonprofit organization called Sogo Way. Its first project was a lively monthly newsletter called *Understanding Japan*. Each month it treats authoritatively, amusingly, and in considerable depth some aspect of contemporary Japanese life, such as education, sports, care of the aged, or changing dietary habits. Before long *Understanding Japan* had subscribers in each of the 50 states and many foreign countries. The Sogos also visit school classes at all levels and undertake Japan seminars for universities.

Not long after their arrival in Denver, Shinsaku and Machiko asked about my interest in writing a book about Shinji Sogo. They told me about his accomplishments, and they said the story of this untypical Japanese who dared to be different would give Americans a deeper understanding of the many faces of Japan. Great idea. But since Shinji was dead, and I do not read enough Japanese to tap library and archival sources, where would I find the raw material I needed? Machiko, who had never met her husband's father, was not to be deterred. She suggested that the basic information would be available in a voluminous book titled simply *Sogo Shinji*. It was written by Sokichi Ariga, a widely known Japanese author, and, the Sogos assured me, he would be happy to cooperate with the project. But of course I was unable to read Ariga's book. No problem, Machiko said. She would translate it for me. So she did, hammering out nearly 500 typewritten pages in three months.

That provided the basic material, but it had to be fleshed out. Some critical information was lacking. For example, Ariga with a deference characteristic of Japanese biographers, skimmed lightly over what I considered the key episode of Sogo's story—the decision to mislead his superiors, in effect his government, about the potential cost of the Bullet Train project in order to get it under way. Since it was impossible to look into Sogo's mind, that episode would have to be recreated from information to be uncovered elsewhere. In 1995, after completing a draft of the manuscript, I went to Japan and spent some time interviewing Mr. Ariga, who turned out to be a delightful old gentleman pleased to have a part in telling the Sogo story to an English-reading public. I also met with Shinji Sogo's other four surviving children: sons Kazuhei Sogo and Rinzo Nozawa and daughters Michiko Kagayama and Keiko Oita and various others, including a number of grandchildren. I discovered to my disappointment that virtually all of Sogo's professional contemporaries were deceased. But the interviews provided insights into the human side of Sogo who, for instance, had a violent temper as well as a tender love for his wife, which he rarely demonstrated. These details enriched the story, and much of the original draft had to be rewritten to provide a more penetrating portrayal.

This additional research also provided a partial understanding of the reason Shinji Sogo chose to mislead his government for what he considered the greater good. Following the great earthquake that destroyed much of Tokyo in 1923, Sogo was in position to help rebuild the capital as a well-planned modern city with extensive roadways, parks, and infrastructure. That would take time and imagination and cost an enormous amount of money. Over Sogo's protests, his superiors chose expedience.

They rebuilt over the ruins, leaving Tokyo little changed from the urban jumble that had grown up on the site of the medieval capital until another disaster, the American firebombings of World War II, destroyed the city a second time. The lost opportunity after the earthquake bothered Sogo deeply. It is understandable that he would risk anything to rebuild his country's railroad system correctly the first time.

This, then, is the story of a remarkable man who, as a traditional Japanese in his personal life but quite un-Japanese in his professional life, had a profound influence on his country at a critical point in its development as a modern nation. Once the manuscript was completed, there was the matter of its publication. Rather than place it in the hands of a trade publishing house, Shinsaku and Machiko Sogo, making decisions always as a team, decided to publish it under the imprimatur of their Sogo Way. Their intention is that it will be the first of a series of books that will supplement the *Understanding Japan* monthly in their goal of bringing about greater understanding between Americans and Japanese. Although *Old Man Thunder: Father of the Bullet Train* carries my byline, more legitimately Sokichi Ariga and Machiko Sogo should be regarded as coauthors.

Bill Hosokawa
Denver, Colorado

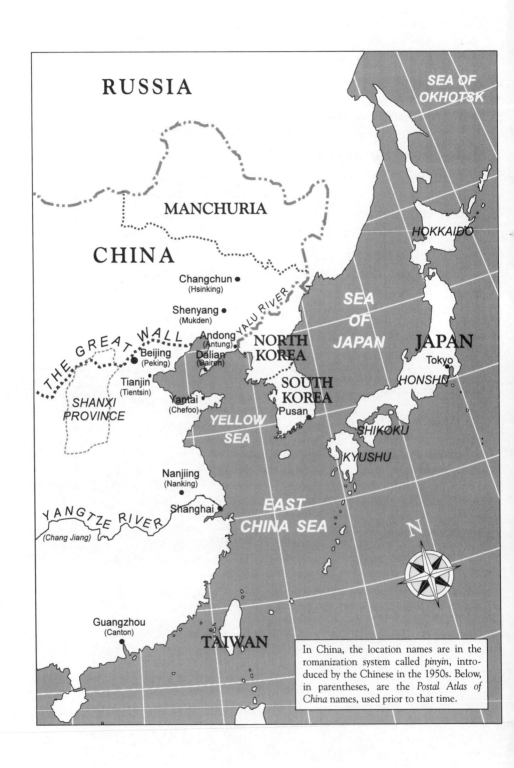

RUSSIA

SEA OF OKHOTSK

MANCHURIA

CHINA

HOKKAIDO

Changchun ●
(Hsinking)

Shenyang ●
(Mukden)

SEA OF JAPAN

THE GREAT WALL

Andong
(Antung)

YALU RIVER

NORTH KOREA

JAPAN

Beijing ●
(Peking)

Dalian
(Dairen)

Tokyo

Tianjin
(Tientsin)

SOUTH KOREA

HONSHU

SHANXI PROVINCE

Yantai ●
(Chefoo)

Pusan

YELLOW SEA

SHIKOKU

KYUSHU

Nanjiing ●
(Nanking)

EAST CHINA SEA

YANGTZE RIVER

Shanghai ●

(Chang Jiang)

N

Guangzhou ●
(Canton)

TAIWAN

In China, the location names are in the romanization system called *pinyin*, introduced by the Chinese in the 1950s. Below, in parentheses, are the *Postal Atlas of China* names, used prior to that time.

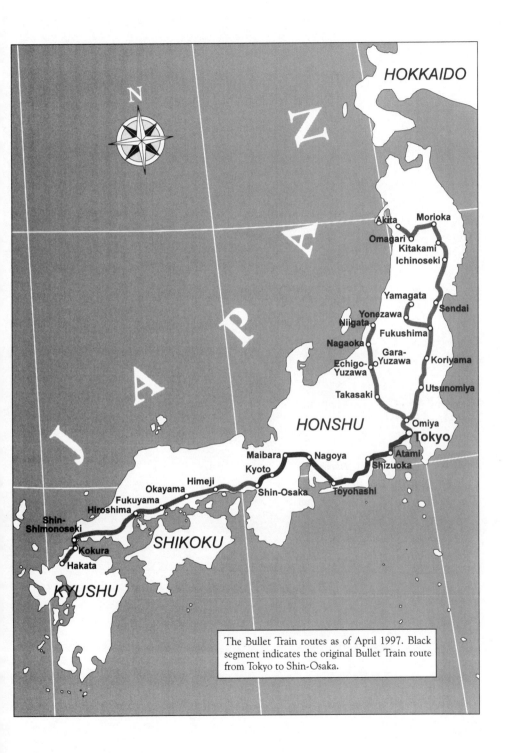

The Bullet Train routes as of April 1997. Black segment indicates the original Bullet Train route from Tokyo to Shin-Osaka.

有法子

CHAPTER 1

THE BIRTH OF THE BULLET TRAIN

At precisely 6 a.m. on the first day of the 10th month of the 39th year of the Showa Era—October 1, 1964—Japan took a giant step that established her position among the world's technological leaders and innovators. In the pale light of morning a half hour before that time, a throng of elderly Very Important Persons in morning coats had gathered on a platform of the newly expanded Tokyo Railway Station to mark the event.

Elsewhere in Tokyo the city was barely coming to life. At the station a band played properly stirring music. Speeches were delivered. White doves were released. Then, at 6 a.m. a ceremonial red ribbon was cut, freeing Hikari No. 1, a sleek, 16-car train nearly a quarter mile long, painted a striking ivory and blue, to head down the track. Its destination was Shin-Osaka (New Osaka) Station, 320 miles distant, where simultaneously a similar ceremony was being performed alongside an exact copy of the Hikari train pointed toward Tokyo.

Everything about both trains exuded a sense of power and speed. Oddly, there was no locomotive, but alternating coaches carried a pantograph that made contact with electric wires overhead. The first car had a distinctive rounded bullet-shaped nose under a rakishly slanted windshield, like an airliner, as did the last car, which gave it the appearance of having to run backward. (In reality the double-ended configuration enabled the train to travel with equal facility in either direction, reducing the turnaround time at the end of a run.) The rounded nose led people to call it the Bullet Train. The Japanese name is *Shinkansen*, which translates into a prosaic "new trunk line," but everywhere else in the world it is the Bullet Train.

The trains' departures on the dot set a precedent for the Bullet Train system's goal of maintaining a virtually split-second schedule. In Tokyo and Osaka 21-gun salutes boomed and loud banzai cheers rose from the assemblage. Almost effortlessly, the trains began to move, and so swift was their acceleration that by the time the last car passed the starting point it was a blur.

Exactly four hours later, Hikari No. 1 glided into Shin-Osaka Station while its counterpart pulled into Tokyo Station. The Bullet Trains had cut the running time between Japan's two largest cities almost in half. They had sped the 320-mile distance, including two-minute stops at Nagoya and Kyoto, at an average speed of 80 miles an hour. Soon, as the brand new roadbed became thoroughly stabilized and the entire system was shaken down, additional minutes were whittled off the timetable.

Today *Shinkansen* and advanced *Shinkansen*-type trains tie the far reaches of Japan together in an amazing network of steel rails. New super express models of the Bullet Trains called Nozomi, departing from Tokyo and Osaka every hour during rush periods, now cover the distance in two and one-half hours—at an average speed of 128 m.p.h. Other trains using the Bullet Train technology race from the northeastern tip of Honshu, the main island of the archipelago, to the southwestern end and there speed through a tunnel under the Straits of Shimonoseki to Kyushu Island's giant industrial complex at Hakata.

In the 30 years since the Bullet Train's first scheduled run, they have covered more than 650 million miles—the equivalent of 1,300 round trips between Earth and the Moon. They have carried 2.8 billion passengers without a single fatality, thanks in large part to a marvelous electronic system that enables technicians in Tokyo to control the movements of every train in the network.

During rush hours on the Tokyo-Osaka route, the passenger equivalent of four fully loaded jumbo jetliners leaves Tokyo Station every six minutes, while an equal number departs Osaka. Many of the passengers are businessmen who are commuting to meetings and conferences in the other city, then returning home for the night. Moreover, the passengers are delivered to efficient city center depots that also serve subway lines, and thus they are able to avoid long taxi or bus rides to and from airports. Equally important to a country that produces no petroleum, the *Shinkansen* requires only one-fifth the energy of aircraft to move an equivalent load.

Creation of the *Shinkansen* system involved much more than competence in railroad technology. Financing had to be arranged. Rights-of-way had to be purchased. Intense political rivalries had to be overcome, for, in addition to national prestige and vast tax revenues, constituent interests were at stake. And various elements of the *Shinkansen* team—civil and railroad engineers, electronic experts, financial specialists, bureaucrats who knew how to make government function but were reluctant to back a horse destined to fail—had to be welded together into a smooth-working mechanism.

There were other important obstacles for the team to overcome. Not least was the national assumption—perhaps a worldwide assumption—that by the middle of the 20th century the railroad era had run its course.

(In 1956 President Dwight D. Eisenhower signed the National System of Interstate and Defense Highways Act that provided the United States with a magnificent national highway system but sounded the death knell of American railroad passenger service. The United States thus committed itself to the convenient but expensive mobility of long-distance travel by automobile and truck. The same year, in the face of considerable public skepticism, the Japanese Ministry of Transportation formed a commission to study traffic demands and the cost of expanding rail service along the Tokyo-Osaka corridor. In the United States 13 years later, 28,800 miles of the projected 40,000-mile interstate superhighway network were open for cars and transport trucks, but 59,400 miles of track had been taken out of railroad passenger service. Clearly, the world's most mobile nation had opted for the flexibility of highway transportation, and many Japanese agreed that was the way their nation also should go.)

Another obstacle for the *Shinkansen* was what might be called Japan's narrow-gauge fetish. All of Japan's railroads were narrow gauge, that is, the rails were 42 inches apart. British engineers who had helped the Japanese build their first rail lines before the turn of the century introduced narrow gauge, which was well suited for the country's mountainous terrain. Japan had stayed with narrow gauge ever since, partly because of tradition but mostly for economic reasons. Narrow gauge was cheaper to build by some 20 percent and required less land for right-of-way. Most Japanese saw no sense in switching to standard gauge (56½ inches between rails), which required building an entirely new system since there was no way to integrate the two.

One of the more vehement opponents of standard gauge was a popular author, railroad buff, and naval historian, Hiroyuki Agawa. In widely published essays he substituted the *Shinkansen* project for the Pyramids of Egypt on his list of history's "Three Greatest Follies." The other two were the Great Wall of China and the Japanese navy's fantastically costly but outmoded superbattleship *Yamato*, which was virtually helpless under attack by U.S. air power. It was sunk by aerial bombs with heavy loss of life (and face) the very first time it engaged the Americans in the waning days of World War II. (Years later Agawa admitted he had been wrong about the Bullet Train and apologized for "lack of foresight.")

On the other hand, engineers counseled that for a new railroad system required to carry heavy loads at high speed, the stability of standard gauge was imperative regardless of cost, and it would be foolish to continue with narrow-gauge design.

The Japanese system of management, amazingly successful in the postwar revival of the economy, is based on *nemawashi*, a word that refers to digging carefully around a tree over a long period, severing only a few roots at a time, to prepare it for the shock of transplanting. In business practice *nemawashi* involves patient negotiation until divergent points of view within a company are modified by argument or compromise into a position that all can support.

Perhaps Japan's need for something like the *Shinkansen* system was too urgent to wait for the time-consuming *nemawashi* approach. And perhaps the issues were too deep-seated and complex to be settled by compromise. Whatever the case, Japan had the great good fortune to put the *Shinkansen* project in the hands of an untypical retired bureaucrat with a big grin, a loud voice, a short fuse, and a reputation for a fearsome temper. His nickname was *Kaminari Oyaji*, "Old Man Thunder." Those who became targets of his wrath were grateful that he cooled off as quickly as he exploded.

Old Man Thunder was a one-time barefoot farm boy who was able to go to college only because of an older brother's sacrifice. He had served his country long and well as a civil servant of unquestionable integrity when, at age 71, he was asked to leave retirement and head the government-owned Japanese National Railways (JNR).

Almost everyone knew the organization was bogged down with huge problems. Two tragic accidents, which had resulted in heavy death tolls, had damaged public confidence. Employees were disgruntled over a number of issues, and morale was low. Although costs were rising far faster than revenues, union leaders were agitating for pay increases. Politicians were demanding new service for their constituencies, regardless of economic feasibility. And somewhere in the not-distant future was a need to do something about increasing the capacity of the Tokyo-Osaka main line. It would take a leader of unusual ability to solve JNR's problems.

Old Man Thunder was an unlikely candidate for the job. He only recently had recovered from a stroke and suffered from severe allergies and extremely high blood pressure. But he could not resist one last challenge even though, as he said, he might die on the railroad tracks. At the time the *Shinkansen* was just an idea within JNR. Still, it played a large part in the old man's decision to take the assignment.

His experience in the bureaucracy had taught him that to carry out his goals for JNR he would have to stomp on many sensitive toes. As it turned out he did not shrink from smashing precedent and alienating the powerful in his single-minded determination to succeed.

But Japanese politics are unforgiving. Just before he could savor the success of the *Shinkansen* project, his official term expired, and immediately after, he was virtually ignored. For a celebration ceremony at the Tokyo headquarters of Japanese National Railways, Emperor Hirohito was present, as was his Empress. So was a bevy of cabinet ministers, politicians, and Railways Ministry officials. Old Man Thunder and his right arm, a gifted engineer named Hideo Shima, were also there, sitting with the lesser guests. In the euphoria of the occasion, hardly anyone noticed them. Although the two men richly deserved to be on the platform when the ribbon was cut, they weren't there, because they hadn't been invited.

Old Man Thunder's real name is Shinji Sogo, and this is his story.

有法子

CHAPTER 2

BIG BROTHER'S SACRIFICE

The Japan into which Shinji Sogo was born on April 14, 1884, was still struggling to emerge from centuries of feudalism. Only 31 years earlier the American Commodore Matthew Calbraith Perry had come knocking on Japan's shuttered doors with his fleet of black warships to invite the shogun warlords into the modern world. Only 16 years earlier, the Imperial Family in the person of 16-year-old Mutsuhito had been restored to the throne to lead the nation in frantic pursuit of the West and its advanced technology.

Despite many important changes, Japan in 1884 still was less a nation than a collection of fiefdoms vying for influence and power in the developing central government established in Tokyo. Children were urged to study hard so they could grow up to serve their country and bring honor to their families and home provinces. "I am going to grow up to become a public servant," the child Shinji told his approving parents.

Shinji was the second son of Nabesaku Sogo and his wife, So-u. Nabesaku was a farmer and, by the standards of the times, fairly prosperous. Their first child was Toranosuke, a boy born in 1877. Then came a girl, Mura, followed by Shinji and another daughter, Shige. They lived in a village called Nakahagi, which now is part of the industrial city of Niihama not far from Takamatsu in Kagawa Prefecture on the island of Shikoku. Today, factories of the Sumitomo group are centered around Niihama.

Shikoku is the smallest of the four main islands that make up Japan and, even now, the least developed. It is a lovely place of low, wooded hills with tiny rice paddies between them. The Pacific Ocean laps its southern shore, and the tranquil Seto Inland Sea, with its sandy beaches where Shinji and his friends often played, is on the north. These beaches were in part responsible for Shikoku's late development. With no convenient harbors, small boats waited a mile or more offshore while passengers and cargo were brought to them in carts pulled by men or horses through the shallow water. The boats then ferried their loads to larger ships waiting to steam to ports on the main island.

Nabesaku Sogo was a commoner, but he could trace the family back to Japan's 12th emperor, Keiko, who according to ancient records ascended the throne in 71 A.D. at age 83. Keiko died at age 143, 137, or 106, depending on the sources one consults. The records also indicate he sired some 80 children, which is also open to question. Among them was Prince Kangushi who built a castle near what is now Takamatsu in an area known as Sogo-machi. The Sogo family fought on the losing side in one of Japan's 16th-century civil wars, and the survivors had to go underground, often changing names and occupations to escape punishment but retaining their family crest, which displays a folding fan atop a table.

"I attended three different elementary schools," Sogo once wrote. "The first was the equivalent of a modern kindergarten. What we did mostly was play and listen to the teacher's lectures. In the rainy season we stayed inside and practiced calligraphy, usually not on sheets of paper but on each other's faces. When we left school, we all looked as black as night."

The second school was near Takeshima Shrine about three miles from home. In adulthood Shinji recalled less about the school than about the summer Drum Festival at the shrine. It was a time of feasting. Shinji's mother prepared special delicacies, and Shinji was allowed to eat some while watching the festivities. He remembered with pleasure the bright red shrimp on seasoned rice sprinkled with aromatic herbs. Young men from neighboring villages, shouting lustily, competed in pulling carriages on which huge drums were mounted. The objective was to crash the carriages into each other, and sometimes the rivalry wound up in gang brawls.

The third school was housed in a former sake warehouse, which, in addition to its pungent odors, was unbearably hot in the summer. Shinji led some of his friends in slipping away from the school grounds to eat their lunches in a cool grove of trees at a nearby shrine, and sometimes, he recalled, they forgot to return to class.

There was no school on Sunday, but it was not a day of rest for Shinji. He was put to work on the family farm. The worst part was transplanting rice from seedbeds into the mud of paddy fields during the spring rainy season. Knee-deep in water, protected from the rain by capes of straw, Shinji and other members of the family bent almost double as they planted the seedlings, one by one, into the mud.

By the time Shinji was ready for middle school, a school was opened in the town of Saijo, about six miles from his home. Since only four years of education were compulsory and classroom space was limited, only the most promising were allowed to continue on to middle school. Shinji was one of them. He and his friends from his village would spend five to six hours a day walking to and from school with nothing but straw sandals on their feet. It is not likely they had much energy for study after so much walking, but they were earnest enough to keep their minds busy by reviewing lessons as they plodded along.

Many of these boys were destined to make their mark in Japanese society, and some of them developed lifelong friendships in school. During part of the time Shinji attended Saijo Middle School, he stayed with the family of an aunt who ran an inn in the town. There he became close to his cousin, Kyoichiro Noma, a quiet and scholarly lad. For some months Shinji and Noma, having been told that morning was the best time to study, would get up early and hurry to school through the winter darkness to take private English lessons from a teacher who had recently returned from the United States. Years later, at Tokyo Imperial University where he was a law major, Noma took an examination on Roman law and gave all the answers correctly in Latin. (Noma became an executive with the Mitsubishi Trading Company, and died in 1937 at age 49.)

Another lifelong friend from this period was Yoshishige Abe, who went on to become a renown Kantist philosopher, minister of education, and president of Peers University. In 1966, two years after the *Shinkansen*'s triumphant inaugural, Shinji Sogo learned Abe had been hospitalized for treatment of cancer. Together with his secretary, Sogo went to see him.

"Mr. Sogo looked into Mr. Abe's eyes," the secretary told friends, "but the two men said nothing, not a word. After a while Mr. Abe said, 'Sogo, I'm fine. Go back to your work.' Mr. Sogo mumbled something like 'Mmmmm' and left the room. They didn't say anything like 'How are you?' or 'Thanks for coming.' They didn't seem to need any words, yet in that quiet time I felt they said everything they needed to say. It was very moving."

Abe died not long afterward.

Such friendships were forged in a school environment that was far from ideal. When Saijo Middle School was opened, many unruly boys from Matsuyama transferred to it. Sogo wrote about those times years later in the *Japan Economic Journal*: "I do not remember exactly when we started, but every year we organized a 'strike.' We wrote down our reasons for striking, signed our names, and submitted the statement to the principal. My name always was at the top of the list, and thus I had to take the paper to the principal. In addition to boy-cotting classes, we got into a lot of mischief. Once in gym class, when we were told to run around the school yard, we dashed off to the beach nearby and held some sumo wrestling matches and even got our teacher involved.

"Students were expected to listen quietly to lectures in class, but quite often I would challenge the teachers with opinions of my own. This would disrupt class discipline. Shortly before graduation I was told the principal had a gift for me, and I was summoned to his office.

"He told me: 'I have never seen such a stubborn, opinionated young man as you. You were able to survive five years at this institution because it is a school. But once you go out into the real world, you will never make it if you do not change your attitude. This advice is my present to you on your graduation.' "

Sogo never forgot the lecture, but it did not change him to any great extent.

Sogo was one of 35 boys graduated from Saijo Middle School in the spring of 1902. Many of the graduates had nothing to look forward to but returning to their homes and entering the family business, which in many cases was farming. But Sogo knew he was headed in another direction, thanks to his brother Toranosuke who had enrolled at Tokyo Technical College, later to become the famous Waseda University.

Toranosuke was doing well in school, but as he neared his 20th birthday he came home to take the examination preceding compulsory military service. He was preparing to return to Tokyo when his father ordered him to forget about school. "As the oldest son," Nabesaku told Toranosuke, "it is your obligation to carry on the family traditions and business, which is farming. You have no need for further education."

Disappointed and resentful, Toranosuke agreed to stay home only on the condition that Shinji, who was considered the bright one of the family, be allowed to go on to a higher education. Nabesaku honored the pledge, and Shinji never forgot his brother's sacrifice.

In the summer of 1902, Shinji left for Tokyo to take the examinations for enrollment at Dai-ichi Kotogakko (better known as Ichiko). Although it was called a high school, it probably was the equivalent of a junior college. There were only six such schools in Japan, and Ichiko was considered the most prestigious. Shinji was one of four graduates from Saijo to apply at Ichiko, and all four were accepted, a fact notable enough to be reported with pride in local newspapers.

Ichiko's reputation as the training ground for national leaders must have awed the country boys from Saijo. The school flag set the tone. It was called *Gokoku-ki*, meaning "flag to defend the fatherland." It had two white lines over a scarlet base and the Chinese character for "country," which was embraced by embroidered gold oak leaves representing the military and literary arts. Assemblies were held in the Hall of Ethics dominated by frowning portraits of two military and literary leaders. The principal at Ichiko was Ryokichi Kano, a mathematics and philosophy scholar, but he was soon to be succeeded by Dr. Inazo Nitobe, whose later writings interpreted Japanese thought and philosophy to the West and whose portrait now appears on his country's 5,000-yen (¥) banknotes.

The faculty was equally distinguished. Sogo's English teacher the first year was Lafcadio Hearn, the American who had immersed himself in Japanese culture and wrote many of the first English-language books about Japan.

Sogo had wanted to study philosophy, but both his father and brother demanded he be more practical. "If you study philosophy," his father said, "the best you can do is become the priest of a temple. Our house is not a temple. I will not send you money if you insist on studying philosophy."

After consulting many professors, Sogo reluctantly decided on a law major because law, although often confusing and mysterious, affected the lives of so many ordinary people. He was one of 80 students who enrolled in the Department of British Law. Among his classmates were Torao Oita (who was to become his best friend and supporter), Yoshishige Abe (the educator who died of cancer), Yukichi Iwanaga (who became head of the Domei News Agency), and many others who were to occupy high posts in the fields of government, education, and politics.

But life in the dormitories belied the dignity and prestige of the school. The first floor of the dormitories was for studying. Sleeping rooms were on the second floor. In some rooms the futon bedding, which traditionally is folded up and put away during the day, was left on the floor, making the rooms look sloppy and unkempt. At night some students, instead of walking to the toilets at the end of the halls, would urinate out the second-story windows, producing what was called "dormitory rain." Sometimes groups of students would harass others by waiting until they fell asleep and dashing noisily from room to room, whooping and laughing in a routine called "storms."

The "storms" forced Sogo, who liked to go to bed soon after supper and get up shortly after midnight, to change his study habits. His appearance changed, too, in keeping with the school tradition that decreed neatness and good looks were unimportant in relation to matters like school spirit and nationalism. Ichiko students affected shapeless caps and wore dirt-gray towels around their waists and shabby straw sandals. Before long Sogo grew a bushy black beard and carried a heavy walking stick. He was nicknamed *Kumako*, meaning "bear cub," perhaps because his movements were so deliberate.

Sogo did poorly in physical education, partly because he was little interested in exerting himself and partly because he hated to hurry. When classes were about to begin, everyone made a dash for the entrance to the gymnasium where shoes were stored. Because some did not own gym shoes, students would grab the first pair available and lace them on. Usually the shoes were all gone by the time Sogo arrived, so he simply would skip class. And although he didn't ask anyone to do it, some student would answer for him when roll was called.

One day the gym instructor discovered what was going on and demanded that Sogo attend the next class. Again Sogo found his shoes missing. He quickly covered his feet with black *sumi* ink to make it appear he was wearing shoes and got into line. "Here, sir," he responded when his name was called. The instructor noticed Sogo's feet and excused him for the day, but failed him when he came to class again with ink-stained feet.

Sogo's allowance from home was ¥8 per month, which was only slightly less than the beginning salary of a police officer. (The value of the yen has fluctuated widely. In the 1930s the exchange value of one yen varied between 25 and 50 cents in U.S. currency. After World War II the yen was pegged arbitrarily at 360 to the dollar. As this is written ¥115 is the equivalent of $1. Japanese currency is on the decimal system, and 100 *sen* equals one yen.) Out of his allowance Sogo paid ¥4.8 per month for meals, ¥1 for his dormitory quarters, and ¥1 for school fees. That left only ¥1.2 for pocket money. (Occasionally, Sogo and his friends would kick in a *sen* or two each and buy baked sweet potatoes from a vendor who came by the dormitories.)

On some university campuses during this period, Japan's policy toward Russia was the subject of lively debate. Many Japanese looked with alarm on Imperial Russia extending its influence from its Pacific maritime provinces into Manchuria and Korea, which Japan considered to be its own sphere of interest. While some left-leaning professors urged renunciation of all war, Ichiko students shared the public's excitement when the Russo-Japanese War broke out on February 10, 1904, and cheered each victory. Russia suffered a series of humiliating defeats and, in the Treaty of Portsmouth in 1905, yielded extensive concessions in Manchuria and Korea to Japan. These concessions were to play a key role in the lives of Sogo and most of his classmates, but few could see into the future. When his class was graduated from Ichiko in the summer of 1905, most of the students moved without fanfare into Tokyo Imperial University, Japan's most prestigious school.

In September 1905, Sogo entered Imperial University's Department of Political Science in the Law School. He must have gritted his teeth to make the decision; general law was one of two classes he had failed at Ichiko, the other being physical education. One reason he had failed the law class was that he had refused to read the textbook, *Elementary Treatise on the Common Law for the Use of Students*, written in extremely abstruse English by an Englishman named Dr. Henry Taylor Terry, because he considered it a waste of time. Realizing the folly of trying to major in a subject in which he had no interest, Sogo gathered some of his friends in a study group to help him with his law lessons. They were lucky to get a young and energetic professor, Kenshiro Kawana, who had just returned from studies in Germany, as their adviser.

Professor Kawana had an almost magical effect on Sogo and his friends. He made law interesting and challenging. The students were excited enough to go to the library for extra research. On Sundays they would meet at Kawana's home to deliver reports and exchange opinions.

In later years Sogo credited Professor Kawana with changing him from a student who hated law to one who found the subject fascinating. "I looked forward to his classes," Sogo said. "I spent time that I should have devoted to other subjects in preparing for his classes. Whatever part law studies had in the success of my career, I owe to Professor Kawana."

有法子

CHAPTER 3

LOVE AND MARRIAGE

In rural Japan at the turn of the century, youths were considered ready for marriage after they reached age 20 and took the army's pre-conscription physical examination. Shinji Sogo was 23 years old and still in his second year at Tokyo Imperial University when his father began to be visited by relatives and friends with the names of young women who might be suitable candidates for him to marry. Of course Shinji, who would be a prize catch, knew little of this. By custom the parents and relatives of a prospective bridegroom had more to say about who he would marry than the man himself.

Nabesaku Sogo had many callers, and he realized he could

not pick a bride for his son without offending most of them. Finally, he threw up his hands and decided to let Shinji break tradition by picking his own wife.

One day, when Shinji came home for a visit, his father told him: "In a big city like Tokyo there must be many nice girls. Pick the one you like best, get married, and bring her back home. I leave the responsibility to you. I cannot stand the pressure from those around me to choose a bride for you. Whichever choice I make will cause friction among the relatives. So do as I say quickly and bring her home to meet us."

Shinji had no job and no income and was dependent on his family for school expenses, but he did not hesitate to do his father's bidding. He had his eye on Kiku Okazaki, four years his junior and a student at Ueno Music Academy in Tokyo. Her father, Choyo Okazaki, son of a samurai family, had traveled to England on a paddlewheel steamer at age 17 to study telegraphy. Back in Japan, he had supervised the laying of the first underwater communication cable between the main island of Honshu and Hokkaido.

Kiku was the first child of Choyo Okazaki and his wife, Tami. Kiku was born in Hakodate on February 21, 1888. She was attending Hakodate Women's College when she told her mother she wanted to go to study in Tokyo. Many years later, Michiko, the oldest daughter of Kiku and Shinji, wrote:

"I wonder what made my gentle mother say that. Maybe because it was the era when Japanese society began recognizing the independence of women, and maybe because the recently developed island of Hokkaido was being influenced by new trends. My grandmother Tami, having three children, was at first confused. But Kiku insisted on going to Tokyo, even if she had to go alone. My grandmother Tami made a decision drastic for the times. She left her husband in Hakodate and took all three of her children to Tokyo so she could make a home for Kiku.

"At the time Western music was new to Japan. Once I heard my mother say, 'When I first heard a Western orchestra I was deeply moved and thought this must be music from heaven.' There was an organ in our home when I was a child, but I never remember my mother playing it. After her marriage to my father Shinji, she completely stopped practicing.

"When my father was a student at Tokyo Imperial University, he must have been either boarding at my mother's house or perhaps living close by. I imagine that he fell in love with Kiku, and because of his straightforward nature, went to her mother to propose. Considering that he was still a student without income, it was incredible to propose marriage. However, an Imperial University student was among the elite of the elite and regarded as someone destined to play a very important role in the future of the nation. My grandmother must have recognized my father Shinji as a man she could trust."

The wedding took place in the spring of 1907. Shinji was 23 years old and a second-year student. Kiku was 19. In celebration, Shinji's father raised his allowance to ¥15 per month. This was far from enough to support a wife. Although the record is not clear, it is likely Shinji moved in with his bride's family.

That summer Shinji took Kiku to meet his family for the first time, but it turned out to be more than just a meeting. While Shinji went back to school, Kiku stayed at his parents' home for nearly a year and a half, until he was graduated. Ostensibly she was being trained in the Sogo family's traditions and way of doing things. In reality she probably was little more than a maid, which was the usual role for a daughter-in-law.

In those days it was common to delay marriage registration, which legalized the union, until the couple had their first child. While Shinji and Kiku were married in the spring of 1907, registration was not completed until September 8, 1908. Their first son, Kosaku, was born October 4, 1908.

(Kiku was frail in her last years but hoped to live to celebrate her golden wedding anniversary. She died July 23, 1958.
"Our marriage lasted 49 years and 10 months," Sogo wrote. "I
was hoping to celebrate our 50th anniversary, but this dream did
not come true. That was our destiny." But figured from the
actual date of their wedding, Shinji and Kiku did indeed live
together for more than 50 years.)

Whatever Kiku thought of living in a country town with her
in-laws while her husband was continuing his education in
Tokyo, she was able to win her father-in-law's approval.

"Kiku is a very good woman," Nabesaku told his son. "I am
proud of you for the choice you made." When Sogo asked why,
his father said: "Kiku has never put on makeup since she came
to stay with us. She did not try to dress up despite the fact that
she has lived in Tokyo and must have been influenced by the
sophisticated life in the big city."

Meanwhile, his responsibilities as a married man did not
seem to make much of an impression on Sogo. He coasted along
at the university, applying himself to subjects that interested
him, and all but ignoring those that didn't. He especially disliked
an economics class—the subject bored him—in which the professor appeared to do little more in his lectures than read from a
textbook he had written. At least that was the impression Sogo
received. He read the book but did not take notes in class. Then,
in the final examination, the professor asked questions that were
not covered in the book. The result was disastrous.

In the spring of 1909 as graduation neared, Sogo ranked
in about the middle of his class. Job-finding suddenly became
important. Because of an economic recession, positions in private industry were scarce, but that didn't worry Sogo. Like
most graduates of the Imperial University, he expected to take
the difficult higher civil service examination and go into a

prestigious government ministry.

One of his advisers was Professor Nobushige Hozumi who made it a practice to take some of his charges to a private club to counsel them on looking for work while teaching them etiquette, like the proper way to eat with a knife and fork. When asked about his plans, Sogo replied sincerely if somewhat pompously:

"I am a son of a simple farmer, but I am about to be graduated from the very best university in Japan. I have an obligation to serve the people who gave me this opportunity. I hope to become a public servant so that I can be of direct service to the people of Japan."

"Well said," Professor Hozumi responded. "You should apply to the Ministry of Agriculture and Commerce."

Shortly, the professor introduced Sogo to officials in the ministry who were favorably impressed. Sogo had a job if he wanted to take it. But before he made his formal application he chanced to meet Kanichiro Matsumoto, an alumnus of Imperial University and a native of Ehime Prefecture, two facts that in Sogo's eyes made him a particularly important person. Matsumoto only recently had left the Ministry of Communications to become a director of the newly established Railway Agency, which had been organized under direct supervision of the prime minister. Its mission was to bring order to a chaotic railroad industry, which was in the process of being nationalized.

"Before you join the Ministry of Agriculture and Commerce," Matsumoto urged, "meet Shinpei Goto, the new president of the Railway Agency. He is an exceptional man, and he is going to make interesting things happen. You won't regret talking to him."

Goto was indeed quite a man. In his early fifties, he had been trained as a medical doctor but had gone into government service. He had distinguished himself as an administrator in Taiwan, skillfully recruiting talented assistants and welding them into a first-rate staff.

After chatting briefly with Sogo, Goto said: "Young man, if you really want to serve the public, you should come to work for the Railway Agency rather than the Ministry of Agriculture and Commerce."

"Sir," Sogo responded, "I have been accepted by the ministry, but if you promise to employ me, I would get permission from Professor Hozumi and decline their offer."

Sogo recalled years later that their conversation went like this:

"How is your school record?"

"It doesn't mean much, does it?"

"Oh, then it must be bad."

"No, sir, it is not bad."

"What is your ranking in your graduating class?"

"I am in the middle."

"That is bad."

"Sir, I do not think so."

"You are ranked only in the middle, yet you say it is not bad. That is arrogance. All right. Can you show me that you can do better?"

"I think that I am fine right now. What more would you like me to be?"

"Can you graduate within the top five? If you do, then I will admit that you are not bad."

Sogo was intrigued by the challenge and excited by the prospect of working for this blunt-spoken man. "Yes, I can," he responded boldly.

Ranking in the graduating class was determined by taking the average of grades in annual examinations and the grade in the graduation examination. Sogo realized he would have to make an exceptionally high grade in the final tests to become one of the top five. His lecture notes were incomplete or nonexistent, and without them he could not expect to do well in the examinations.

Sogo borrowed notes from his more diligent friends and studied all night before the exams while they slept. When the grades came back, Sogo was second in his class in the graduation tests and fifth overall.

"Sir," Sogo reported to Goto, "as you requested, I have become the fifth-ranking student."

"Don't try to fool me," Goto retorted, but he was extremely pleased.

In July 1909, Sogo became one of 10 law graduates hired by the Railway Agency. Until then the railroad industry had put a priority on employing engineers. Goto obviously anticipated a need for administrators. Instead of being put to work, Sogo was told to study for his higher civil service examination, which was scheduled in November. He passed the tests with the ninth highest grade nationally. Of the oral part of the examination on criminal law, Sogo wrote:

"The test was given by a famous professor, Kanzaburo Katsumoto of Kyoto Imperial University, and I was the last applicant of the day. On the question of the difference between fraud and larceny, Professor Katsumoto and I got into a heated debate about proprietary rights. I argued that the precondition of the debate, regarding the rights of ownership in civil law, was misinterpreted by his theory, and therefore many of his conclusions were misleading. He disagreed. Our discussion continued after 5 p.m. Finally Professor Katsumoto said, 'It's getting late. Which way are you going?' It turned out we were taking the same tram, so we continued our discussion as we rode until we said goodbye at a stop near his home."

有法子

CHAPTER 4

HARD LESSONS ABOUT RAILROADING

Administrative problems in getting the new Railway Agency under way had persuaded Shinpei Goto that he would need management specialists. Many private railroads had been built with little regulation during the rush to modernize after Japan was opened to Western influence in 1864. At the same time, the government also undertook railroad construction. By 1906 the government owned and operated two systems with about 1,500 miles of track, while 38 privately-owned railroads totaled about double that length of trackage.

The war against Russia had demonstrated the importance to the nation of a reliable transportation network under direct government authority. If most of the privately-owned lines had acted in their own best interests, there were well-based fears that in a crisis the government's hands would be tied. Nationalization was seen as the logical way to give the nation complete authority over the rail system.

Attempts to nationalize quickly ran into political and economic barriers. As one example, coal production on Kyushu Island was dominated by the powerful Mitsui interests, but Mitsui was at the mercy of the rival Mitsubishi's railroad for transporting its output. Mitsui used its influence with mine operators and political leaders to promote nationalization of railroads in anticipation of cheaper rates, while the equally powerful Mitsubishi conglomerate threw its influence behind opponents of nationalization.

So controversial was the issue that Foreign Minister Takaaki Kato resigned in protest after the Diet approved nationalization. It was not incidental that Kato was the son-in-law of the founder of the Mitsubishi conglomerate.

The Diet voted 214 to 0 to pass the nationalization bill, but the figures do not tell the whole story. When the vote was called for, opponents staged a violent demonstration before walking out. The lower house consisted of 379 members, but only the 214 in favor of the bill cast ballots.

Under the bill two existing government agencies, the Imperial Government Railway and the Railroad Bureau of the Ministry of Communication, were abolished and replaced by the new Railway Agency. As an official but independent entity, the Railway Agency presumably would be free from the influence of the various ministries. The agency was authorized to buy, over a 10-year period, 17 of the most important privately-owned railroads with a total of approximately 2,900 miles of track. Later the term was shortened to two years because of controversy over which of the railroads to buy and in what order. The new

Railway Agency also was given jurisdiction over the South Manchuria Railway (Mantetsu), which had become Japanese property under the Treaty of Portsmouth ending the war with Russia. As the spearhead of Japanese economic development in Manchuria, Mantetsu was a powerful political force.

Under the consolidation, the Railway Agency was required to employ many executives from the companies it had absorbed as well as tens of thousands of workers. It was no easy job integrating them into a single system. Shinpei Goto, who had performed brilliantly as civil administrator of Taiwan ceded to Japan following the Sino-Japanese War in 1895, and as first Japanese president of the South Manchuria Railway, faced many knotty problems. "I was told that I was the only person who could organize the Railway Agency," Goto once said immodestly, "and I had no reason to discourage this impression."

Sogo reported for work at this difficult time and found 17 or 18 factions in the Agency, none of them trying very hard to get along with the others. President Goto was in the process of firing deadwood and replacing them with bright young men like Sogo. Within months after he took charge, Goto got rid of some 3,500 workers including 75 high-ranking officers. Within the next year he had fired another 1,300.

Sogo's first assignment was the general affairs section of the accounting department. His starting salary was ¥40 per month. He found more than a dozen factions in that department alone, each group using the accounting system it had been employing before the consolidation, and none paying any attention to the new fellow fresh out of college.

Shortly after he reported for work Sogo was summoned to meet President Goto. Goto frowned when he saw that Sogo was still wearing the heavy beard and mustache he had affected at school. Beards and mustaches were fashionable in Europe and the United States at the time, and the Japanese, who generally have sparse facial hair, considered such adornments admirable among those in power or authority. The growth on Sogo's face should have been an asset, but on the other hand he was just a youth.

"As you know, I am the president," Goto reminded Sogo, "yet I keep only a small beard and mustache. You are just a young employee, yet you wear a mustache and beard covering your whole face. What impudence! Shave it off!"

Too young to know better, Sogo replied: "Sir, I am just following the teachings of Confucius who tells us our bodies are precious gifts from our parents. Not to hurt our bodies is the first thing in returning something to our parents."

"There is no room for argument," Goto roared. "This is an order. Shave it off."

The next day Sogo appeared for work with only a small mustache.

For most of his first two years at the Railway Agency, Sogo was a frustrated young man unable to utilize his talents. His section chief gave him no meaningful work. He and the other law graduates exchanged notes and found all had been told to sit next to their section chiefs and watch what was going on. They consoled each other by organizing a "club" they called Fuurin-kai, *fuurin* meaning "wind chimes which were visible but accomplished nothing." A half year after he went to work, Sogo was told that unlike engineers hired at the same time he had no idea how a railroad was run and he would be assigned as a station trainee to learn the jobs of conductor and maintenance man.

Sogo protested. "We should not disturb men carrying out responsible operations by unsystematic on-site training," he argued. Nonetheless, he was ordered to six months of duty in the railroad finance office in remote Nagano, a city in the mountains some distance from Tokyo. Two days later he was back in Tokyo.

Instructed to explain himself, Sogo revealed both youthful arrogance and independent good sense. "I am a graduate of Tokyo Imperial University, where I had to study very hard," he said. That was something of a fib, but he went on: "I was given time off with pay to prepare for my higher civil service examination, which I passed with honors. Now I have been assigned to Nagano as a trainee for six months without responsibilities. Two days of observation in Nagano were enough to learn all I need to know. I have come back because I do not believe I need further training. I am asking for assignment at some meaningful work. If I cannot perform adequately, fire me."

His supervisor's response was not encouraging. "You will do as I tell you," he said. "Sit next to my desk and observe what I do. If you get bored, you can read the newspapers."

At this late date, it is not possible to tell whether Sogo's boss intended to punish him or just wanted to get this difficult young employee out of the way. Whatever the reason, Sogo commuted to the office every day with his lunch wrapped in a *furoshiki* cloth and spent his time reading newspapers and magazines.

When Sogo complained to a friend, he was advised to do what he was told. He also was urged to read two books written by Englishmen on railroad operations and railroad economics. As he struggled through the books with the aid of a dictionary, Sogo for the first time began to understand the financial side of the railroad industry. "It was an eye-opening experience," he admitted later. "The books gave me an understanding of what the railroad business was all about."

Shinpei Goto had many ideas about what the Railway Agency should be doing, but unfortunately he seemed unable to articulate them to his underlings. It might not be inaccurate to say he expected aides like Sogo to absorb his thinking simply by observation.

Goto had been hospitalized for a month before he took over the presidency, and he used the recovery period to outline five points of the policy he would follow:

1. Delegate authority to section chiefs. Since they know what needs to be done, they should be free to run their sections. Put another way, it was an invitation to cut red tape.

2. Place highest priority in the areas where the work is being done. In other words, place responsibility in branch offices.

3. Be good to employees and take care of their needs.

4. Provide workers with all the tools and supplies they need to do their job.

5. Promote better communication between management and labor. The Agency, with 90,000 workers, needed to grow into a close-knit organization.

At another time Goto laid down four principles, some of which duplicated his earlier points.

1. Do not be bureaucratic. Goto anticipated that when the nationalization process was completed, workers from the private sector would lose their initiative and settle into comfortable bureaucratic habits, and he was anxious to prevent that.

2. Keep the railways out of politics. This was an impossible goal, since new railway routes and building priorities were always election issues. In a developing country, railroad expansion almost inevitably became a political issue. In elections, where and when new lines would be built became a bargaining tool. Goto insisted that the Railway Agency must not be allowed to become a political pawn.

3. Maintain harmony with trust and team spirit. His immediate job was to weld the personnel and business habits and philosophies of 17 private companies into one government agency. Goto wanted all of them to think of themselves as members of the Railway Agency "family."

4. Modernize Japan's railway system by switching from narrow to standard gauge. Goto believed Japanese railroads would never reach adequate efficiency without adopting international standards.

(When construction on the present Tokyo Station was begun in 1910, the ground was found to be soft and waterlogged. More than 10,000 pine logs, many as much as 25 feet long, were brought in. Some were cut from forests standing on ground now occupied by the Imperial Hotel in the heart of downtown Tokyo. Crews of female construction laborers, hauling on primitive rope-and-pulley piledrivers, stood the logs on end and pounded them into the ground. Concrete was poured over the logs to support the foundation. Nearly 60 years later, the logs were found in good condition when excavated during a reconstruction project. But once the logs were exposed to the air, they rotted out within six months.)

Despite its problems, the nationalized rail system prospered until the devastating earthquake of September 1923 destroyed a large part of the Tokyo-Yokohama metropolitan area. Before the system and the national economy could recover fully, Japanese armies became involved in Manchuria and North China, drawing off resources needed to expand and modernize the railroads. World War II and the decade that followed was a period of emergency, chaos, and reconstruction, leading to 1964, which opened the brilliant *Shinkansen* era.

Sogo could see the merit of Goto's goals, and somehow or other he absorbed them into his own management philosophy. But not before continued difficulties. In April 1910, Sogo's supervisor was replaced. Sogo thought his situation might change, but months passed and nothing happened. Discouraged, Sogo finally went to President Goto to submit his resignation.

Explaining that he had accomplished nothing, Sogo said:

"I am grateful for the opportunity you gave me to work for the Railway Agency, but I am afraid I have failed. I have accomplished nothing. There is no work for me here, and I cannot stand to waste my days like this. I ask your permission to leave the Railway Agency as of today."

Goto replied with a smile: "When I told you I would give you a job that others were not willing to do, you said you were ready to bear any hardship. Have you given up already?"

Goto continued: "You do not need to work for the accounting section any longer. From now on you will do what I ask you to do. In the near future human relations—the relations between people, between management and labor—will become a critical matter. Labor issues will be a big problem. Beginning today, you will study problems that will arise between the company and its workers, particularly salary and social welfare needs, and how they relate to the Agency's ability to realize the profits necessary to improve and expand its services."

Goto explained that he was planning to build a hospital to care for workers and their families and to form a mutual aid association where employees could go for advice about personal problems, borrow money at low interest rates in time of need, and get help in times of sickness or injury.

"We now have 96,000 employees," Goto said. "Most of them are dedicated to their work, the organization is becoming more solid, and the railway business is prospering. But in Europe and the United States, progress has been impeded by strikes. The damage from these strikes is enormous. People who manage railways should never stop trying to reduce workers' worries and complaints. They should create a good working environment to prevent strikes. Your special attention to these matters would be very much appreciated."

For the first time Sogo understood that Goto was grooming him for top-level management responsibilities, that he had to learn to take orders, that he had to be patient, that he had to demonstrate his ability to accept discipline. In something of a daze, Sogo left the president's office. His days of reading news-papers on the job were over.

有法子

CHAPTER 5

Introduction to America

Almost before he could get started on his new assignment, Shinji Sogo's career ran into another roadblock. On December 1, 1911, he was called up for one year's military service. He was inducted as a corporal, the lowest noncommissioned officer rank, in the paymaster's section of the First Guards Infantry Regiment.

Normally, compulsory military service was for two years, but men with a middle school education or higher could shorten their term of service by making a monetary payment.

Sogo was 27 years old. He had two children, son, Kosaku, who was 3 years old, and a 17-month-old daughter, Michiko. To fulfill his military obligation, Sogo had to take leave without pay from the Railway Agency. To make ends meet, Kosaku was sent to live with his mother's parents, and Sogo's wife, Kiku, returned to Niihama with little Michiko to stay with her in-laws. It is not likely that the village women, who were still smarting that Sogo had chosen to marry Kiku instead of one of them, were very cordial. Michiko was too young to remember that experience, but she recalls her mother telling her it was very helpful that she was a good girl.

"Being a woman in the Meiji Era," Michiko says, "it is likely my mother never complained about her situation. But I assume it must have been the hardest period of her life."

It undoubtedly was. On his corporal's pay her husband could send her no money. Despite her earlier stay with her in-laws, Kiku was a city girl accustomed to big-city life. If the people of Niihama were not openly hostile, the little country village must have been completely boring.

Meanwhile Sogo, too, was trying to make the best of a not particularly pleasant situation. Even though his primary duty was to see that his unit was paid, Sogo had to go out almost daily on exercises. In the dead of winter the men would leave their barracks in the Kudan section of Tokyo, run through the city, skirt some frozen paddy fields, scramble through a forest to the banks of the Tama River, and then trot all the way back. Years later he recalled the most frightening experience was to climb the stone wall of the Outer Palace in Tokyo in full equipment.

"Neither the stones nor I were stable, and just thinking about what would happen if I fell made me tremble," he said. Some mornings, before embarking on drills, the men would do their laundry in icy water and hang their clothes out to dry. When they returned, as often as not they would find their wash scattered on the ground. It was their squad leader's way of expressing his displeasure with their performance.

But as in all armies, the enlisted men found ways to get back at their officers. Sogo discovered that while it was extremely difficult for individual soldiers to get permission to leave the barracks, a unit could march out without being questioned. Sogo and some of his friends took turns forming impromptu "units" which they marched out the gate after supper with loud commands on their way to their favorite bars.

"I was not a good soldier," Sogo wrote years later. "I did not obey orders, and I sometimes avoided carrying out my duties. It was very unusual for a graduate of Tokyo Imperial University to finish his military service without a promotion, but because of my attitude I left the army at the same rank at which I entered it—a corporal. But the time was not all wasted. The experience I had was a great help later in my career when I had to deal with the military. My year in the army proved very valuable."

Sogo received his discharge on November 30, 1912. Only eight days earlier the second cabinet headed by Prime Minister Kinmochi Saionji fell over an issue involving expanding militarism. War Minister Yusaku Uehara had proposed a bill authorizing the creation of two additional army divisions. His argument was that Japan needed more troops to tighten its grip on Korea, to meet the anticipated threat of a united China after the Chinese Revolution of 1911 led by Dr. Sun Yat-sen, and to counter Russia's increasing presence in eastern Siberia. These were issues about patriotism and national destiny the public could get excited about. The line between aggression and defense was not easy to distinguish.

Pleading lack of funds and unwilling to raise taxes, the Saionji cabinet rejected the bill. War Minister Uehara resigned in protest. At the time the constitution specified that only top-level active duty officers could serve as army and navy ministers. In effect, the military services could exercise veto power over national policy simply by withholding representation in a cabinet. When the army refused to nominate a successor to Uehara, the entire cabinet had no choice but to resign.

Taro Katsura became the new prime minister, and he appointed Shinpei Goto to serve as his minister of communications as well as continuing as president of the Railway Agency. Burdened by his new duties, Goto had to restrict the time and energy he could devote to the Railway Agency.

That is the situation Sogo found when he returned to his desk. Working diligently to make up for the time he had lost, Sogo began to understand what a huge and complicated organization the accounting section was, and what an opportunity Goto had given him to learn all about the government's railroads. In addition to budgeting, the section was involved with employee salaries, labor-management relations, and even had a role in purchasing decisions.

But it was hard to concentrate on routine duties when Japan was in turmoil. A wave of nationalistic patriotism was sweeping the country. Tens of thousands of rightists demonstrated in the streets of Tokyo demanding the ouster of the Katsura government, which was no more willing than its predecessor to fund additional army divisions. Five thousand police officers were called out to disperse the demonstrators. Mobs set fire to police kiosks.

Mounted policemen rode into the crowds in a futile attempt to scatter them. Only Katsura's resignation quieted the country. For the first time citizen power had toppled a Japanese cabinet. Sogo was among the young bureaucrats who, caught up in patriotic fervor, vowed not to wear overcoats as a gesture of sacrifice, or buy a new one, so they could contribute to a fund to finance the army's expansion.

The swing to the right went beyond a cabinet change. At the Railway Agency a new director reversed Goto's policy of delegating responsibility to local offices. Power was returned once more to the tight-knit group of administrators at headquarters.

Early in the spring of 1916 Sogo was chosen, along with several other junior executives including his friend, Torao Oita, to spend a year in the United States. He was told to study railway administration and finances, particularly in the fields of "expenditure and storage." However, such assignments were loosely interpreted. The real purpose of the program was to give promising young bureaucrats the experience of living in a foreign country. The reports they were required to file usually went unread.

The participants were to be given transportation costs and the equivalent of $100 per month for expenses, and their families were to receive one-third of their regular salaries. Sogo felt he could manage to live in the United States on $100 monthly, but he was unwilling to force his family—he now had three children—to exist on one-third of his salary, which by then had reached ¥150.

(His first son, Kosaku, was born in 1908. His daughter, Michiko, followed in 1910. His third child, Kenji, a boy, died soon after birth, and another son, Rinzo, was born in 1916. They were followed by two more boys, Kazuhei in 1920 and Shinsaku in 1929, and a daughter, Keiko, in 1926.)

Reluctantly, Sogo told his supervisor that he could not afford to accept the opportunity of going abroad. Then he requested and received permission to postpone the assignment for a year while he got his finances in order.

For the next year Sogo worked harder than he ever had worked. After office hours he tutored, taught classes, and took on manuscript translation for publishers. Within a year he saved ¥2,000, the equivalent of 14 months' salary.

On February 23, 1917, fortified by a number of letters of introduction, Sogo set sail from Yokohama for San Francisco. His destination was New York City. His contact there was

YMCA Senior Secretary John F. Moore, who looked after rail-roaders stopping at the "Y" residence. Apparently one of his duties was to befriend foreign students. At a farewell party Sogo had expressed concern that some day the United States and Japan would go to war against each other. Explaining that while he wanted to learn about politics, economics, and railroad operations in America, Sogo also said, "I will study hard to find out what Japan must do in order to meet the possibility of war."

At this time it is impossible to say whether Sogo really believed war was a likelihood, or whether the evening's drinks had fueled his bravado. World War I was raging in Europe, but the United States was still not directly involved. America was to become a combatant only months after Sogo arrived in New York. Whatever the case, by the time Sogo had been in the United States for any length of time, he was more interested in learning about American family life and attitudes toward religion and education than assessing the nation's war-making potential.

Moore, the YMCA secretary, introduced Sogo to Genevieve Caulfield, an unmarried woman slightly older than Sogo, who had been blind since childhood, to practice conversational English before he went to live with an American family. After a few days she asked Sogo: "What is your impression of American women?"

"Not good," Sogo replied. "I don't like the way they behave. They are nothing compared to the gentle Japanese women."

She asked: "How many American women friends do you have?"

Unabashed, Sogo said, "The only women I have talked to in New York, besides you, are two waitresses at a coffee shop."

"I feel rather responsible for your unfavorable impression of American women," she said, suppressing a smile. "I am going to introduce you to a family you might like."

(In 1968 Sogo received a letter from Ms. Caulfield mailed from Saigon. She said she had established the Bangkok School for the Blind in Thailand, was still active at age 82, and happened to be in Vietnam. A few days after the letter arrived, the Vietcong launched its massive Tet Offensive against U.S. and Vietnamese forces. Sogo tried to reach Ms. Caulfield in Saigon but learned she had left for Bangkok only a few days before the attack.)

Sogo's hosts were Dr. and Mrs. William Diller Matthew and their three children, who lived in suburban Hastings-on-Hudson. Dr. Matthew was a renown paleontologist at the American Museum of Natural History in New York City. After their modest dinner, Dr. Matthew made it a habit to read in the living room while Mrs. Matthew, sitting at the same table, mended the family's clothing. It was a tranquil domestic scene that impressed Sogo.

Breakfast usually was oatmeal and coffee. After a few days of hesitation Sogo asked why there was no sugar. Dr. Matthew explained they were conserving sugar so it could be sent to the troops in Europe.

"Is this a law or some kind of government regulation?" Sogo asked.

"No," Dr. Matthew replied. "It is neither a law nor a regulation. Our government leaders have told us of the need to conserve sugar, and we, as American citizens, are limiting our sugar consumption voluntarily."

Sogo was impressed. He had thought that, unlike the Japanese, Americans would not make sacrifices for their country.

One Sunday afternoon Dr. Matthew, wearing a military uniform and carrying a rifle, was about to leave the house. Sogo asked him where he was going.

"Our town has only one police officer," Dr. Matthew

explained. "Those of us too old to serve in the army have formed a home guard, just in case there is an emergency. We bought uniforms and guns at our own expense, and Sundays we hold drills under former military officers."

"After getting to know Dr. and Mrs. Matthew I felt ashamed," Sogo admitted, "for having thought Americans were only money-worshipers, that American women thought only of pursuing luxury, that the people were arrogant. I was impressed that in a crisis everyone, without being ordered, would bear inconveniences. Such an attitude was all new to me."

After several months Sogo moved to Rochester, New York, to study a small, local railway company. Soon after he arrived, he received a letter and small parcel from Mrs. Matthew. The letter said she was sending something of his that she had found while cleaning his room.

Sogo was quite sure he had not forgotten anything. He opened the parcel and found a pair of his socks. They were old, and he had worn holes in them. Sogo had been using the socks to clean his shoes and had forgotten to throw them away when he left. He found that Mrs. Matthew had washed and darned them before sending them on.

Sogo blushed with shame. At the same time he was filled with gratitude. He wrote to Mrs. Matthew: "I am speechless in trying to express my appreciation. Your kindness has made the socks too precious to wear, I will share the story with my wife, and we will keep the socks as a reminder of the lesson in kindness you have taught me."

It was in Rochester that Sogo saw a unit of local soldiers marching to the railroad station on their way to join their outfit. As they swung down the street Sogo was astonished to see a young woman dash out of the crowd and kiss a soldier. "She must be insane," Sogo said to himself. But soon there were other girls running into the street to kiss the soldiers, and no one seemed surprised. "How can effete men like this fight a war," Sogo wondered. But later he learned the local unit had distinguished itself in combat.

From Rochester Sogo moved to Jersey City, New Jersey, where for two months he lived in the home of Henry L. Austin, an executive of the U.S. Steel Corp. They lived in a mansion near a park, and Sogo was given use of a large bedroom called the Green Room. Mrs. Austin was interested in Japan. The day Sogo arrived she invited friends and relatives to view her collection of Japanese art. Sogo was called on to demonstrate how to make ink on an inkstone and write with a brush on paper as it was unrolled. While everyone marveled at his skill, he proved less than dexterous at dinner when a piece of chicken he was trying to cut skidded off the plate onto the floor. The next day Mrs. Austin started Sogo on lessons in table etiquette.

Mrs. Austin took Sogo to visit a high school class studying current affairs. The discussion was about French and British envoys who were in the United States seeking a larger American commitment of troops, supplies, and money for the war against Germany. When Sogo was asked what was being sought by a Japanese delegation that had just landed in San Francisco, he replied:

"I don't know about the ambassador, but all I want from you is friendship." Obviously his views had changed from the time when he was expressing fears about war between the United States and Japan. Years later, talking about his first visit to the United States, Sogo said:

"At every home Americans accepted me as a member of the family. When I had the wrong idea about Americans or things American, they kindly corrected me and tried to explain the situation until I understood.

"I learned far more than I expected about American attitudes toward education, religion, and family life. My stereotyped views about Americans were shattered. It is said there are no national boundaries for people's hearts, and what I experienced in America showed the truth of this saying. Among educated Americans, I never felt racial discrimination."

(Early in 1981 Sogo received a letter from Harrison Finch, a retired Trans World Airline captain. It said in part:

("In or about 1922 you were in the United States studying American railroads. You were in DuBois, Pennsylvania, and, I believe, a dinner guest at the home of William Irving Finch, then chief clerk to the superintendent of motive power of the Buffalo, Rochester, and Pittsburgh R.R. I am his son.

("Neither my sister Hilda nor I have forgotten you. The cards that you sent my father and the book on the hot springs of Japan are still in our possession. I recall my father's attempts to get in touch with you after the 1924 earthquake, and when he failed, it was assumed you had perished.

("I am now retired, having flown as a pilot with Trans World Airlines for 33 years. My father died in 1947, my mother in 1968. Recently I volunteered to assist a museum in Pennsylvania recover some World War II aircraft abandoned in New Guinea and in this capacity had occasion to talk with Colonel Ninomiya of the Japanese Embassy in Washington, D.C., and asked about you."

(Eventually Finch learned Sogo was still living and wrote to him. Finch concluded his message with: "This letter is to tell you that we have not forgotten you, and that your cards and book are still looked at with pleasure, and to extend the good wishes of the Finch family."

(A short while later Finch received a warm and appreciative reply from Shinji Sogo's son, Shinsaku Sogo. It said Shinji Sogo was now 97 years of age and hospitalized. "Since my father is in rather serious condition," Shinsaku wrote, "I have not been able to tell him about your letter. I'm sure it will make him very happy when I do tell him.")

It would make a good story to report that Sogo recovered enough to be told of Finch's letter and that he remembered his visit to the Finch home. Unfortunately Sogo died a few months later without knowing.

The American experience changed Sogo in important ways. He discovered that while Americans were friendly toward him, they held a similarly friendly view of Chinese, who generally were looked down upon in Japan. Many Americans were upset by what was known as Japan's "21 Demands" which, in 1915, initiated the policy of subordinating China and laid the groundwork for Japanese domination of the Chinese mainland. In 1917, somewhat to the discomfort of many Americans, these demands won tacit U.S. support in the Lansing-Ishii Agreement under which Washington recognized Japan's special interest in China and Japan pledged maintenance of Chinese territorial integrity, independence, and the "open door." Sogo recognized the need for Japan to keep an understanding relationship with the Chinese, an attitude that influenced him as his stature grew. He understood that good relations between Japan and China, politically and economically, were the key to better U.S.-Japan relations.

It was fortunate for Sogo that he was able to stay in American homes. Many later visitors from Japan stayed at a Japanese-run inn in New York called Kokumai, literally meaning "national rice," where they ate Japanese food and did not have to use English at all.

How good was Sogo's English? Like most Japanese who have studied the language, he could read it quite well. But speaking was another matter. Shortly after his arrival in New York, he was at a YMCA conference when without notice he was asked to say a few words. He recalled that during the five minutes he spoke he had to stop several times and ask to be excused while he thumbed through a Japanese-English dictionary in search of the right words.

In Rochester he told a somewhat skeptical audience: "In Japan, when we get paid, we give our entire salary directly to our wives, and we receive an allowance from them as we need it." A member of the audience asked Sogo to speak at his church, which he did. Afterward, Sogo asked his hostess, Mrs. Smith, whether she thought the audience understood him. She replied in a kindly manner: "I understood you very well, because I talk with you face-to-face every day. But I wonder if the other people could."

有法子

CHAPTER 6

MOVING UP

Early in the spring of 1918, Sogo was living at the Kokumai Inn in New York when he received a cablegram ordering him to wind up his affairs and return to his office. His year in America was up. It was a message he had been dreading because, weeks before it came, he had run out of money, even the funds necessary to get to the West Coast to catch his ship. He had been spending most of his days reading newspapers in his room because he had no cash to do anything else. Swallowing his pride, he cabled Tokyo explaining his plight and asking for more funds.

Before receiving a response he was visited by Naoharu

Toda, another young Railway Agency employee. Toda came from a wealthy family which kept him supplied with spending money. Sensing Sogo's problem, Toda pressed a roll of bills into his friend's hand and said, "Please use this to buy the medicine you need." Sogo accepted gratefully.

Not long afterward Torao Oita, who had arrived in the United States a year earlier than Sogo but had been given permission to extend his stay, came to New York from Chicago. Sogo met him at the station, intending to take him to a good restaurant with Toda's money.

"I'm starved," Oita said. "I ran out of money and traveled all the way from Chicago with nothing to eat. Let's go to the closest place. Anything is fine." So the friends went to the nearest diner and enjoyed a cheap meal together.

Sogo's travel funds finally arrived, and he reached Japan on August 10, five months after his scheduled return.

His daughter, Michiko, as an adult remembered that her father brought her a thick mail-order catalogue as his gift from America. She was fascinated by page after page of pictures of household items, furniture, clothing, toys, and books. "I looked through the catalogue day and night," she said. "My mother was not pleased that he failed to bring me something special, but I was totally happy. The catalogue opened a new world for me, and I dreamed of visiting America someday."

(That dream did not come true until many years later. When one of her sons-in-law moved to New York on a business assignment, Michiko visited for a month. Her daughter and son-in-law took her on a tour of New England where she attended village festivals and visited schools and historic sites. She was particularly pleased by a visit to the setting for Louisa May Alcott's book *Little Women*, which her father had given her.

(Michiko has mixed memories of her father. She remembers him as a thoughtful, loving parent as well as someone who, completely engrossed in his work at times, neglected his family. She recalls that in childhood he bought her expensive books, mostly translations of European and American fairy tales, which her friends did not have. When she applied for entrance to a prestigious girls' high school, he rather than her mother accompanied her. But much of the family's attention was centered on her little brother, Kazuhei, who was a sickly child. Once, when Sogo raised his voice for some forgotten reason, Michiko recalls asking her mother, "Why did you marry such a tyrant?" Her reply: "He works and studies very hard to improve himself.")

Immediately after his return Sogo was assigned as a section chief in the general affairs department. Although he had little opportunity for input, Sogo in his new position was caught up frequently in the continuing controversy over whether Japan's narrow-gauge rail system should be converted to standard gauge. In essence, the issue was money—how a limited supply should be spent to the nation's greatest advantage. But it was inevitable that the controversy should become a durable and volatile political football with important local and national implications.

Japan adopted a narrow-gauge system in the first place on the advice of Edmund Morel, a British engineer who arrived in 1870 to supervise construction of the nation's first railroad. Apparently Morel, who had helped build railroads in South Africa and New Zealand, believed narrow gauge was preferable because it was more flexible in negotiating Japan's mountainous terrain. It also may be Morel was aware that British manufacturers had surplus narrow-gauge locomotives and rolling stock, originally meant for South Africa, that they were anxious to sell. It has been said that the Japanese officials who accepted Morel's recommendation did not understand the advantage of one gauge over the other, but agreed to narrow gauge because it was less expensive to build and thus the young nation could get more miles of track for the same expenditure.

This line of thought continued to dominate the position of narrow-gauge advocates. Various localities throughout Japan were demanding rail service, and politicians were under great pressure to provide it. This led to construction of some rail routes that zigzagged from one town to another or looped in a huge half-circle through several towns instead of linking two population centers in a direct line. In the language of a later era, it might be said that narrow gauge provided more political bang for the buck. The Japanese had a saying: "Build a bridge and a politician is assured of reelection for three years; get a railroad and he is in for life."

On the other hand, opponents of narrow gauge contended that Japan's rail system could never operate with efficiency comparable to foreign railroads unless standard gauge was adopted. Their primary concern was to increase the capacity of main lines to move greater loads at higher speed—to serve the needs of the military as well as industry—instead of building unprofitable new lines into remote areas.

But there was another dimension to the financial pinch. The problem wasn't only about extending the rail system versus improving the capacity of the existing system. Around the ever-expanding metropolitan population centers, there was also a growing and very expensive need to double-track existing commuter lines, upgrade passenger cars, and improve speed, service, and safety.

One argument used by opponents of standard gauge was the cost of converting existing lines as well as the higher cost of building new standard-gauge lines. Advocates countered by citing the experience in Manchuria where railroads were standard gauge. At the end of the Russo-Japanese War the retreating Russian army took all their rolling stock with them. The Japanese army had to ship narrow-gauge locomotives and cars—which was all they had in the homeland—to Manchuria and then convert the rails to accommodate them. When the South Manchuria Railway reopened for business under Japanese management, narrow gauge was reconverted to standard gauge. The whole reconversion job, covering hundreds of miles of track, was completed in a year and a half, demonstrating the relative ease with which gauge could be changed.

Countless studies and reports were made about the advantages and disadvantages of continuing with the narrow-gauge system in the homeland versus converting to standard gauge. While Sogo was in the United States, his mentor Goto had ordered two experiments. In one, a new rail was laid on each side of a set of narrow-gauge rails. In the other, an extra rail was laid at one side of the conventional rails. Trains were run over the tracks to demonstrate that conversion by either mode would not be difficult or expensive. The tests also indicated that the entire fleet of passenger and freight cars could be converted to standard gauge within 10 years, but for opponents of conversion that was too lengthy a commitment.

The issue was so heavily politicized that each new cabinet seemed to reverse the decisions of its predecessor. This practice produced some bizarre results. The mile-and-a-half-long Hirase Tunnel in the central mountains of Honshu was drilled to accommodate narrow-gauge trains at both ends, and standard gauge in the middle section, reflecting changing orders as the work progressed.

In 1919, two years after Sogo's return from the U.S., the Railway Agency was upgraded to the Ministry of Railways headed by a cabinet minister. Sogo was promoted to chief of the first purchasing section, and shortly after that to chief of the accounting section. In that job he was responsible for buying rolling stock, rails, bridge girders, construction and maintenance equipment and machinery, and other items made of metal. His monthly salary was raised to ¥340, nearly five times that of a new employee who had passed the higher civil service examination. Sogo was now 35 years old and had overcome much of his early truculence but little of his drive. His promotion, in which for the first time a nonengineer was given a key managerial position, marked the opening of a new era in the government's railway agency.

Sogo was aware that he knew little about purchasing. He couldn't expect much help from the men in his department, most of whom were career paper-shufflers. He could learn about purchasing by studying the books that were available, but engineering knowledge was too technical to be acquired by casual reading. How could he determine the best materials and equipment to buy without input from trained engineers? Some of his staff, who had settled into a bureaucratic "do nothing and there will be no mistakes" mode, resented the youthful Sogo's efforts to shake up the department. Once, after a department party in which liquor had flowed freely, some chief clerks tried to pressure Sogo into easing up on them. His patience at an end, Sogo smashed a bottle against a table and demanded they back off. He had no more trouble after that.

Sogo spent much time visiting factories of suppliers and kept a file of evaluation cards. Nor was he too proud to invite advice from outside experts. One of them was Enzo Ota, a young engineer who was considered something of a genius and who was to prove invaluable to Sogo as he moved up the promotion ladder.

Not long after Sogo's promotions, Railways Ministry executives were summoned by Shinpei Goto for an announcement that an aggressive expansion policy had been adopted. The meaning was clear; expansion meant narrow gauge. Goto's speech sounded almost like a requiem for his personal efforts toward converting to standard gauge. "I regret that I could not attain my goal," he said, "but I still believe in the merits of broad gauge. I hope you will continue your efforts to achieve what I know is best for Japan."

Sogo, while he still endorsed Goto's goals, threw himself into preparations for the expansion move ahead. One of his first steps was to buy an American IBM machine for analyzing statistics that he had seen in the U.S. It was far superior to anything Japan had. Up until then employee salaries had been analyzed by entering figures by hand on cards. The work was slow, laborious, and often inaccurate. The IBM machine completed in several days work that had taken up to a year.

There was other American equipment that Sogo knew would be useful, but he realized he needed an adviser. It was unprecedented for a government section as small as Sogo's to hire a foreign adviser, but he found an American, a Dr. Millner, and put him on the payroll anyway. Millner promptly earned his pay by advising Sogo about the merits of powerful new construction machinery—electric hoists, pneumatic rock drills, huge concrete mixers, giant pumps, and steam shovels—being built in the U.S.

Sogo established contacts with suppliers, and when the equipment was needed he knew where to get it.

After his promotion, Sogo and Torao Oita, with whom he had discussed the idea in New York, organized an informal group called the Kayo-Kai (Tuesday Club) made up of young executives. They met every Tuesday afternoon at the Tokyo Station Hotel for informal discussions about their work. The meetings were strictly informational. No conclusions or recommendations were reached, but the executives kept each other aware of what was going on in other departments of the Ministry of Railways. Thus they were well prepared when their superiors brought them policy papers for comment.

The issue of discontinuing first-class service is an example of how Kayo-Kai influenced railway policy. Aside from a few well-heeled foreign tourists, only a handful of the privileged—mostly politicians who had free passes—rode first class. On the other hand, third-class cars, usually packed with the common people, provided 90 percent of the passenger income. In 1920, first-class cars were discontinued except on two main lines used frequently by foreign tourists, and third-class service was improved. When a member of the House of Peers told the press of his plan to restore first-class service, Kayo-Kai blocked the movement by threatening to reveal other privileges being enjoyed by politicians.

Kayo-Kai members were the first in management positions to become aware of the growing strength of the railway union. Top management's idea for discouraging unionism was to give workers places where they could meet and relax, and where leaders of workers' committees could sit down with managers to discuss mutual problems. Sogo and Oita, having become familiar with the more aggressive American labor unions, were skeptical. They argued that committee meetings were only a halfway measure, and that the foundation for smooth labor relations was unions that could meet with management on the basis of equality. But nothing came of their suggestions, and top officials were shocked when they learned one day that the Great Japan Locomotive Workers Union had been organized and was demanding recognition.

When pressure was put on senior Railways Ministry officials to disband Kayo-Kai because it was "disrespectful of senior officials," Sogo as spokesman replied: "We would be happy to change if we only knew what it was that you wish us to change. Please tell us specifically what it is that you don't like about Kayo-Kai and the reasons why and how we can please you." That was the last time Kayo-Kai heard about disrespect.

One of the few centers of relative tranquility in Sogo's life in this period was the Saijo Student Dormitory established in

Tokyo. At this period in Japan's development, the scores of clans scattered throughout the country were still competing for influence and prestige in the new society. Their brightest young men were being encouraged to go to Tokyo—as Sogo and his friends had done—to further their educations and prepare to work into positions of power. A Saijo Association had been formed in Tokyo to aid students from the Saijo area. One of its projects was a dormitory where students could find a home away from home and get the kind of supervision that would help in their studies and provide assurance for parents.

The first Saijo Dormitory was a house rented in 1913. Some years later the association built a dormitory building large enough for 20 students, and Sogo was asked to move into an adjoining home as housemaster. Perhaps remembering the often chaotic times he experienced in school dormitories, but also tempted by the rent-free quarters, Sogo took on the responsibility of looking after the students in addition to his regular job.

Despite his youth, or perhaps because he was young, Sogo was able to build a close rapport with the boarders. Each month he held a meeting of all Saijo students to hear their complaints and views, and to dispense some fatherly advice. "Continue studying even after you leave school," he urged. And drawing on his own experience, he would add: "Good politics places the right person in the right place at the right time." He set an example by reading for several hours every night, even when duties kept him late at the office. And he was up early. Even though the students were still asleep, he would hit a tennis ball against the storm doors, making so much noise that the boys would have to get up and play with him.

On hot summer weekends Sogo and Kiku enjoyed serving watermelon sprinkled with wine. Some Sundays Sogo would take the students to pick strawberries. Over the New Year holidays students who were unable to go home became part of the

Sogo family for the traditional feasting. Kiku mothered the boys, slipping them spending money when they were short. Her graduation gift to each boy was a dress shirt so he could be properly attired when job-hunting. Twice a year Sogo would take the boys on a trip to some historical site or scenic resort.

"I had a rich friend, Ryohei Matsuhashi, who made a lot of money in the securities business," Sogo explained. "He offered me funds to use in promoting education. I was following his wishes when I took the students on educational trips."

This innocent practice eventually got Sogo into trouble, but that is getting ahead of the story.

有法子

CHAPTER 7

EARTHQUAKE EMERGENCY

In the summer of 1923, Shinji Sogo was instructed to prepare for a two-and-a-half-month trip to China with Counselor
Kiyoshi Kanai of the Railways Ministry. Sogo was pleased. He
had never been to China and was anxious to learn how the
Chinese ran their railroads and the impact railroads had on
the nation's economy.

Departure was set for September 2. On the previous day,
shortly before noon, the last of the documents necessary for
travel was delivered to Sogo's office in the Tokyo Station
building. He slipped it into a briefcase with other important
papers and returned to his desk stacked with materials that

required his attention before leaving.

A few minutes later, at precisely 11:58 a.m., the earth heaved in a mighty convulsion under the deep, dark waters of Sagami Bay about 50 miles from Tokyo. Swiftly, the shock radiated outward from the epicenter. A giant tsunami raced for shore. In Tokyo and Yokohama steel and concrete buildings danced before they crumbled to the ground. Office structures, factories, homes, and bridges collapsed. Gaping cracks appeared in highways, and railroad lines were ripped apart. Touched off by cooking fires and sparking utility wires, flames licked up through the debris. Gas lines exploded. Unchecked, fires spread swiftly through the ruins. Before the conflagration could be brought under control, nearly 200,000 lives were lost—crushed by the wreckage, burned to death, washed out to sea and drowned, even swallowed up by an earth suddenly gone berserk. Tokyo Imperial University's seismometer registered the quake's intensity at a staggering 7.9 on the Richter scale.

Tokyo Station suffered little damage, but the Railways Ministry's main building in the Gofukubashi area caught fire that evening and was destroyed. The Saijo School Dormitory and Sogo's home nearby were not greatly affected. As soon as he learned his family had escaped injury, Sogo's next thoughts were about the railroad system. How badly had it been damaged? What needed to be done to restore service and transport relief supplies and relief workers into the stricken area? But there was no way to find out until communications could be restored.

There is no good time for a disaster, but the Great Tokyo Earthquake could not have come at a worse time. Prime Minister Tomosaburo Kato had died on August 24. Gonnohyoe Yamamoto was designated as the new prime minister, and he was still in the process of trying to assemble a cabinet when the quake struck. Tokyo citizens were in a panic. Medical facilities were jammed. Martial law had to be imposed and food and water distributed. The government had to allay fears that it would flee out of Tokyo, perhaps permanently. And once the emergency needs had been met, there was the staggering problem of reconstruction.

Finally, three and a half weeks after the earthquake, the Yamamoto cabinet established a Capital Restoration Agency to direct the rebuilding of Tokyo and Yokohama. Shinpei Goto, Sogo's old mentor who had been named Minister of Home Affairs in the Yamamoto cabinet, was appointed to head the new agency.

Sogo had not waited for the government to act. The first reports to his office were devastating. Aside from heavy damage throughout the Tokyo-Yokohama area, the main trunk line to population centers to the west—Nagoya, Kyoto, Osaka, Kobe— had been severed near the foot of Mount Fuji. It might take anywhere from two to six months to get the trains running again. Shiploads of food and medical supplies were dispatched to the stricken area from western ports the day after the quake, but there was still a great need for ground transportation.

As an emergency measure Sogo proposed buying a fleet of trucks from the United States. After a quick conference of department heads, Sogo was authorized to cable an order for 1,000 vehicles to the Ford Motor Company for delivery within a month. If anyone had wondered what they would do with the trucks after the emergency, Sogo had an answer. He would start a delivery service within the Railways Ministry, trucking light freight from railroad yards to the consumers.

As soon as Goto was established in his new office, he asked that Sogo be loaned to his agency during the emergency. His job would be manager of the railroad engineers who, because they were most qualified, would be assigned to rebuild highway bridges as well as rail lines. Sogo would have preferred to stay in the Railways Ministry because it faced huge reconstruction jobs, but he could not refuse his former boss. He agreed to the transfer on the condition that Enzo Ota, whom he liked and respected, would be made director of engineering.

Goto, who knew Ota by reputation, agreed without hesitation. But two days later, when appointments were announced, Ota was listed as an assistant to the director of engineering, Rintaro Naoki. Sogo immediately asked Counselor Kanai, who was familiar with personnel matters, what was going on and was told Naoki had been named at an executive meeting because of his seniority; he was a former official of Home Affairs, and besides, he was older than Ota.

Furious, Sogo demanded an immediate meeting with Goto. Sogo was told the minister's daytime schedule was completely filled, and since he was entertaining he would not be available until midnight. Sogo and Kanai were kept waiting until 1 a.m. By then Sogo was seething.

He told Goto: "I agreed to work for you because I believed you are the only man with the vision and administrative skills to rescue Tokyo from chaos. I trusted you and your judgment. Now I find you are like everyone else, making appointments on the basis of seniority and the year the candidate was graduated from college, and not on ability. You agreed with me when I told you Ota was best qualified for the responsibility. Now you have gone back on your word. I am disappointed in you. I cannot work for you any longer if you doubt my judgment and break promises."

The maturing Sogo was far different from the youth who had agreed meekly to shave his beard when admonished by Goto. Sogo was demonstrating the firmness of character that Goto had detected when he first agreed to hire the college student with mediocre grades. In total violation of Japanese business etiquette, Sogo had not hesitated to speak out in opposition to his superior when he felt an important principle was at stake. After he made his point, Sogo stalked out of Goto's home, realizing that perhaps his insubordination meant his career in government was over.

It was 3 a.m. when Sogo reached home. He wrote a curt letter of resignation, instructed his wife Kiku to post it by registered mail in the morning, and walked out into the night without knowing where he was going. He wound up at Tokyo Station, took the first morning train, and finally found himself in Ikaho, a tranquil village and hot-springs resort in the mountains west of Tokyo. Sogo took a room at an inn, rested a while, then went for a walk in the forests nearby.

Presently he heard someone calling his name. It was Enzo Ota, the engineer over whose appointment Sogo had risked his career.

"How did you know where to find me," Sogo asked.

"Don't forget Mr. Goto is the Minister of Home Affairs," Ota said. "He has ways of finding people."

In those days railroad conductors and stationmasters kept track of prominent people on their trains and notified stations ahead of the presence of VIPs. It was a simple matter for Goto to locate Sogo.

Ota said that after Sogo left the minister's residence, Goto telephoned some of his associates including Naoki, the chief engineer designate, and told them what had happened. They agreed that Sogo had a point, that he and his railroad engineers were essential to the rebuilding of Tokyo, and Naoki agreed to take a lesser position. Early the next morning a messenger was sent to Sogo's home only to find he had disappeared. That was when Ota was ordered to find Sogo and give him the news.

Back at his office the next day Sogo received two official letters. One said his visit to China had been canceled. The other was his appointment to the Capital Restoration Agency.

Goto had ambitious plans for rebuilding Tokyo. He wanted the government to purchase the devastated area in downtown

Tokyo at an estimated cost of ¥4.1 billion. The landowners would be paid with interest-bearing bonds which could be kept or sold. The entire area would be bulldozed and the cleared land sold or leased for redevelopment. The main attraction of such an idea was that downtown Tokyo would be planned and rebuilt as a modern metropolis. Tokyo had been no more than a medieval city crisscrossed with tiny alleys and narrow, winding streets more suited for rickshaw and bicycle traffic than for motor vehicles. Additionally, its water, sewer, and power systems were completely inadequate.

The idea of building a new Tokyo fascinated Sogo who also had been listening to Dr. Charles A. Beard, a historian and professor of political science at Columbia University who had been invited to Japan as a consultant. Beard's proposal was to clear the ruined area and plan a transportation network before allowing any permanent structures to be erected. "Rebuild the city not for today, but aiming at eternity," he advised.

Goto's idea was so staggering that, predictably, it ran into powerful opposition. One concern was the huge amount of money involved. A second was the need to restore Tokyo and Yokohama as quickly as possible and revive the national economy. Some of Goto's most influential friends argued that his plan was too idealistic, and that it was more practical to improve water and sewage facilities, restore the old road network, and get houses and office buildings up as soon as possible. Others contended that ownership of land was a sacred right and those deprived of it should be compensated with cash rather than with bonds that could fluctuate in value.

Goto could see that his proposal was getting nowhere when the Finance Ministry proposed a reconstruction budget of ¥1.2 billion, only a little more than one-third of the amount he had sought. Of that sum, ¥720 million was to go to the Restoration Agency and ¥500 million to be divided among various other ministries. Ultimately the Diet agreed on a total of ¥510 million, only one-eighth of Goto's proposal.

Five months after the earthquake, the Restoration Agency was abolished as an independent entity and reconstituted as a minor bureau within the Ministry of Home Affairs. With that decision died a great opportunity to rebuild Tokyo as a 20th-century city.

(On the premise that the old Tokyo had to be leveled before it could be rebuilt, Japan had a second opportunity to modernize its largest city when vast sections were destroyed by incendiary bombs dropped in American B-29 raids in the closing weeks of World War II. In one night attack in March 1945, an estimated 100,000 Tokyo residents died in the raging fires. Again, the need to rebuild quickly—plus a treasury depleted by the war—prevented orderly redevelopment. Nearly two decades later, as Tokyo spruced up in preparation of hosting the Summer Olympic Games, main thoroughfares were widened at enormous cost, elevated highways constructed, and flimsy older structures gave way to handsome new buildings. Sections of downtown Tokyo in the 1990s are impressive collections of architecture, but as Dr. Edwin O. Reischauer has pointed out, roads occupy only 12 percent of its area compared to 35 percent in New York City.)

Faced by the budget limitations, Sogo had to proceed cautiously in purchasing heavy equipment and machinery and supplies, such as steel, cement, and lumber. Ota also wanted to hire American engineers to help with design and supervise construction. Sogo went so far as to ask the Audit Bureau whether the salaries of foreign engineers could be included as the cost of machinery. The answer, of course, was no.

The stress of trying to do the best possible job with an inadequate budget weighed heavily on Ota. In building bridges over the Sumida River that flows through Tokyo, Ota asked a number of artists to submit sketches of what they considered beautiful spans. Then he invited writers, philosophers, artists, and architects to comment on the renderings. Finally he chose five and asked bridge designers to put together plans based on the sketches. The bridges that Ota built are now called the Eidai, the Kiyosu, the Komagata, the Azuma, and the Kototoi. Even today they are graceful, sturdy, and utilitarian, but they rise out of a hodgepodge of warehouses, factories, and nondescript dwellings.

Two and a half years after the earthquake, on the night of March 21, 1926, Ota was at home reading a drama written in English when suddenly he rose and killed himself. He left no note of explanation, not even a will. He was only 45 years old. Perhaps he can be included among the Great Tokyo Earthquake's delayed victims.

Meanwhile, Sogo was having problems of his own. Budget cutbacks made it necessary to reduce the payroll and exercise even greater caution in purchases. When Mitsugu Sengoku became railway minister, he ordered the next year's construction budget slashed from ¥80 million to ¥30 million. Some opposition party politicians protested loudly that there was no provision for new lines into their districts. Even some employees of the Ministry warned that such a drastic reduction would compromise the safety of the railroad system. But Sengoku was adamant.

One day Sogo was sent to the Ministry of Finance to explain how the new budget would affect operations. Sogo's instructions were to meet with the vice minister, since Sengoku himself was planning to talk to Finance Minister Yuko Hamaguchi. After Sogo had completed his explanation, the vice minister said: "This plan doesn't appear to be feasible. What do you think?" Sogo replied honestly: "I agree. With the drastic cuts made in the budget, railroad safety may be at risk." The vice minister asked Sogo to share his views with Minister Hamaguchi. Sogo explained that he had been told Minister Sengoku would be talking personally to Hamaguchi, but he was taken to Hamaguchi's office anyway. Hamaguchi asked numerous questions about Sogo's views and got some honest answers. Finally Hamaguchi told Sogo: "You are right. The budget should not be slashed so drastically. You do not have to report this conversation to Sengoku since I am going to talk to him myself."

A few days later Sogo was summoned before an angry Sengoku. "Don't you understand the role of a messenger?" Sengoku demanded. "I sent you to the Ministry of Finance to explain our plans for a budget, and you gave your own opinions to the minister. Did you forget that I told you I would be conferring directly with the minister?"

"Sir," Sogo replied, "I met the vice minister and reported our decision as you instructed. Then he asked for my personal opinion. I had to be honest. I told him what I thought."

"That is unacceptable," Sengoku retorted. "You should not have told him."

It was Sogo's turn to be angry. "Then why did you send me?" he asked. "If you want your messenger to act like a recording, one of the junior clerks could have done the job. You sent me because you wanted someone who could respond appropriately when questioned, and I gave them honest answers."

Sengoku brushed that aside and reminded Sogo he had been told there was no need to talk to the minister.

"I was aware of your instruction," Sogo replied. "I told the vice minister, but he insisted I meet with Minister Hamaguchi. In responding to the minister's questions, I was very careful to differentiate between the Ministry's official position and my personal opinion. Whatever conclusions the minister reached were on the basis of his findings. I answered his questions. I did not try to influence him in any way."

Sengoku's face broke into a grin. "You did the right thing," he said. "I understand." After that Sogo was called frequently into Sengoku's office to give his opinion about policy matters.

有法子

CHAPTER 8

THE BRIBERY SCANDAL

The Japanese parliamentary system, like the British, requires cabinet ministers or their designees to appear before the Diet periodically to report on their activities and be questioned about them. On January 26, 1926, Shinji Sogo, representing Railways Minister Sengoku, was in the the Diet building waiting to testify when without warning he was seized by officers of the Tokyo District Public Prosecutor's Office and hustled off to Ichigaya Prison. There was no announcement as to the reason for the arrest. However, bribery scandals in connection with the Capital Restoration Agency were much in the news, and there was speculation that Sogo was involved.

In those days government officials appearing before the Diet wore formal morning dress. A *Mainichi Shimbun* reporter who witnessed the arrest noticed that the lining of Sogo's coat was badly worn. Later he said he felt instinctively that any government official who wore such old clothes could not have taken bribes.

In the absence of an official announcement about reasons for the arrest, newspapers the next day were full of speculation. One story reported Sogo's office and private residence had been thoroughly searched by the police. Other stories said the director of the criminal affairs division had indicated charges against Sogo were not serious and he would be released soon.

The most telling report indicated Sogo had been made the pawn in a high cabinet disagreement. The story said Tasuku Egi, minister of justice, and Matsukichi Koyama, the public prosecutor general, were feuding. Since the high-profile Sogo could expect to be under investigation routinely as were many others, one published report indicated some of Egi's enemies arranged for Sogo's arrest in a ploy to embarrass the minister.

News of Sogo's arrest stunned his friends. His boss, Railways Minister Sengoku, urged him to regard the indictment as though it were a natural disaster over which he had no control. Sengoku said that when he heard an investigation was underway, he assured Egi that Sogo was not the kind of man who would even think about taking bribes. His old friend Torao Oita was distraught and among the many who demanded to testify on Sogo's behalf. But there was little anyone could do because under the system then in effect the prosecutor's office did not have to reveal the charges until a formal court appearance.

Meanwhile, Sogo was being grilled daily by Oka Ishigo, known for his relentless questioning. Hour after hour he was asked about friends and associates in the business and political arena. Eventually Sogo became upset and protested:

"Prosecutor, the way you ask questions it sounds as though you know all the answers before I can reply. What are you trying to drive at?"

"I have to be suspicious, because you have so many friends in companies that you made purchases from," Ishigo said. "After all, friendship is about money, isn't?"

Sogo turned livid. "Friends are gifts from heaven," he replied, trying to hold his temper. "I don't make friends for convenience. I do not become friendly with someone with the intention of making money. People who cultivate friendships with profit in mind are bandits. True friendships are bound together by heartstrings."

"Heartstrings," the prosecutor sneered. "Don't mock me by talking about friends being tied together by heartstrings. Young lovers may whisper to each other about hearts, but I know what you have done, and you cannot escape from me."

Sogo raised his voice. "You and I live in different worlds," he told the prosecutor. "I have no way to understand what you are up to. You are misusing your power as public prosecutor. I do not know what kind of proof you have of wrongdoing, but I refuse to cooperate with you any further."

Sogo was moved to a house of detention where he was kept for 37 days with almost no contact with the outside world. Under regulations, Sogo was suspended from duty by the Railways Ministry on the day after his arrest, January 27, 1926. Two days later he was discharged and dropped from the payroll.

Sogo's family at the time consisted of his wife Kiku, sons Kosaku, 17, Rinzo, 10, Kazuhei, 6, and daughter Michiko, 15; Kiku remained stoic, but the children were mortified. For days Michiko refused to go to school. Sogo had been living on his monthly salary and had almost no savings. Most of his bonuses were spent on the students at the Saijo Dormitory. Old friend Torao Oita was aware of this. Each payday he called on Kiku

Sogo and left half his pay. Even after Sogo was released from prison pending trial, Oita continued to share his salary. Sogo accepted the money with sincere appreciation, but between the two men there was no sense of borrowing or lending money. As true friends, they simply were sharing. For the first two months at the detention house Sogo was kept idle. Since he had not been told of the charges against him, he was in no position to plan a defense nor could he consult an attorney. Over and over in his mind he reviewed all his activities at the Ministry. There was not one thing he could think of that would be considered illegal or morally wrong.

The questioning started again during his third month in detention. Then abruptly on May 3, 1926, he was told he could post bond and go home. When the news circulated, one of the first to call was Shinpei Goto. "Congratulations," Goto said. "I am glad you are home. You have experienced enough to qualify as a full-fledged man." Frequently after that Goto would take Sogo out to dinner and send him home in the minister's official car, a clear signal of confidence that no one could overlook.

The case against Sogo finally came out in the open with the start of the trial in late summer. He was charged with receiving bribes in four specific cases connected with his duties in the Railways Ministry and the Capital Restoration Agency:

1. When after the earthquake he bought certain parcels of land in Tokyo to be cleared in order to speed up road reconstruction.

2. When he imported lumber from the United States, Canada, and Southeast Asia for postearthquake reconstruction.

3. When he bought land in Ito, a town in Shizuoka Prefecture, on which to build a hospital and other medical facilities for railroad employees.

4. When he purchased rotary converters for the Railways Ministry power plant.

In addition he was charged with improper financial dealings with a former Railways Ministry employee named Ryohei Matsuhashi who had become wealthy speculating in the stock market. Let us examine the evidence that came out in each of the bribery charges.

The charge that Sogo took a bribe in the Tokyo land purchase case was the flimsiest. In August of 1924, Kennosuke Inaba, director of a government department involved with land-clearing operations, was arrested and accused of having accepted bribes. During the investigation Inaba indicated he had acted under orders from Sogo, but the prosecution was unable to link Sogo with any payoff.

The lumber case was more involved. The prosecution contended Sogo accepted bribes to buy 12 million *koku* (one *koku* is a fraction less than 10 cubic feet) of timber from the United States and Canada. Actually, the order was placed by the Ministry of Agriculture and Commerce in anticipation of reconstruction needs before the Capital Restoration Agency had been formed. After Sogo joined the agency he discovered that the proposal was to buy 3 million *koku* from the U.S. immediately. Perhaps recalling his impulsive decision to buy 1,000 Ford trucks (which had been cut back to 300 vehicles), Sogo estimated the lumber order was far more than was needed or could be utilized in a reasonable period and should be cut back to 1 million *koku*.

"What do you know about lumber?" Goto had asked when Sogo proposed the reduction.

"Nothing," Sogo replied. "I'm just following my instincts."

"Then let the order stand," Goto said. "Lumber specialists have endorsed 3 million *koku*. The decision has been approved by the cabinet and the House of Peers, and anyway the order already has been placed."

"There's another problem," Sogo said. "There is no way we can consume so much lumber quickly and no place to store all those logs after they are delivered. The sea around Yokohama will be filled with logs, and if they are kept in the water any length of time they will be covered by barnacles and other sea growth, and they won't be much good for anything. If we store the logs on land until they can be cut into lumber, there will be a high rate of decay. If we try to sell the logs too quickly, the bottom will fall out of the market and the government will take a heavy loss. Why can't we cut the initial order to 1 million *koku* and be prepared for additional orders when needed?"

Reluctantly, Goto gave Sogo permission to see what he could do about slashing the order. He ran into opposition from both Americans and Japanese. After much negotiating, the U.S. agreed to ship a first order of 800,000 *koku*, Canada 200,000 *koku*, and Southeast Asian countries 50,000 *koku* of hardwood for furniture. Even with the smaller shipments Sogo was under constant pressure from the private sector to put surplus logs on the open market. It was understandable that Sogo's complicated maneuvering in the lumber market should raise the prosecutor's suspicions about bribery.

The founding of a railroad employees medical facility had been on Sogo's mind ever since Goto suggested it as a project at the time Sogo was ready to quit the Railway Agency because he had been given nothing meaningful to do. Near the end of 1922, top officials at the Railroad Ministry were approached by the mayor and city council chairman from the town of Ito, not far from Atami, a well-known seaside hot-springs resort. The Ito officials said they understood the Ministry was looking for at least 10,000 *tsubo* in Atami where land was scarce and expensive. Why not, they said, look at Ito where there were several possible sites and land was much less expensive.

Sogo was among those taken to Ito on a site inspection tour. They found several likely pieces of land. After getting the opinion of engineers and architects, the Ministry bought a piece of land. Now the prosecutors were charging that the Ito city government could not account for ¥5,000, with indications that the money was given to Sogo to influence the sale. Much later it was discovered the money had been pocketed by a member of the city council, and Sogo was not involved at all.

The fourth charge was even more complicated. It stemmed from the Railways Ministry's decision in 1925 to install heavy electrical devices called rotary converters in their power stations at Kawasaki, Ueno, and Shiodome. American firms like General Electric and Westinghouse manufactured high-quality rotary converters, but the Ministry decided to purchase domestic models to boost Japan's post-earthquake economy. The lowest bid was ¥539,000 from Hitachi, followed by ¥560,000 from Shibaura (now Toshiba) and ¥663,000 from Sumitomo.

Neither Hitachi nor Sumitomo had experience in building rotary convertors. However, the Ministry of Railways gave part of the contract to Hitachi because its bid was the lowest and part to Shibaura because of its experience. And because of its factory capacity and its location close to the power plants where the converters would be installed, Shibaura was given the major share. Shibaura's sales manager was a man named Hirasawa who was a good friend of Ryohei Matsuhashi, the former Railways Ministry employee who had become wealthy in the stock market. Testimony brought out that the Shibaura Company gave Hirasawa ¥23,000 to be given to Matsuhashi, presumably in appreciation for his part in influencing Sogo to do business with Shibaura. However, further investigation showed that Matsu-hashi received only ¥9,000 with Hirasawa pocketing ¥14,000. Hirasawa told investigators he was prepared to give the money to Sogo whenever he asked for it. Sogo had met Hirasawa on a number of occasions, but there had never been any mention of a payoff, and no money had changed hands.

Sogo had become acquainted with Matsuhashi in 1909

when Sogo entered the Railway Agency as a trainee. Sogo was confused by the numerous factions within the agency, and Matsuhashi was helpful in showing him the routine. After a year Sogo, who had a higher civil service rating, was named Matsuhashi's supervisor. Matsuhashi lost interest in his job, and his work deteriorated. Sogo tried to encourage his friend, often inviting him to dinner to talk about their work, and eventually Matsuhashi earned a promotion.

While Sogo was in the United States, he received a letter from Matsuhashi saying he had enjoyed considerable success in the stock market and planned to leave the Railway Agency to go into the securities business fulltime. Later Matsuhashi said he had made a substantial profit by investing in sugar companies and would be happy to contribute to Sogo's work at the Saijo Dormitory.

Sogo had just been paid ¥2,000 for some work he had done in New York for a Japanese company importing iron ore. "Please invest this money for me," he told Matsuhashi. "I don't know anything about investing, so just treat it as though it were your own money." From time to time Matsuhashi brought modest sums which Sogo spent on the Saijo Dormitory or gave to students.

At the same time Sogo was having other financial problems. His brother, Toranosuke, had quit farming and tried other businesses. He had managed an orchard and run a porcelain factory and a glass manufacturing plant, but all of the ventures failed. Each time he came to Shinji for help in settling his debts. Shinji still felt obligated to Toranosuke for the opportunity to get a higher education, but he did not have the money to give his brother much assistance. It was brought out in court that Shinji Sogo had borrowed ¥12,200 from Matsuhashi, of which ¥11,200 had gone to Toranosuke and ¥1,000 to the Saijo School. The prosecutor contended the money Sogo received was a bribe, not a loan.

Finally, on June 29, 1927, the Tokyo District Court returned its verdict. Sogo was found guilty of receiving bribes from Shibaura in the purchase of the rotary converters and receiving other bribes from Matsuhashi. He was sentenced to serve six month in prison and pay a fine of ¥12,200. The sentence was suspended for three years.

Sogo immediately filed an appeal. A petition attesting to Sogo's character, signed by 75 prominent Japanese business and political figures, was presented to the Appeals Court. Kyoichiro Noma, the cousin with whom Shinji had lived while attending middle school, took leave from his post as head of Mitsubishi Trading Company's office in Berlin to testify. In a hearing before the Appeals Court, Torao Oita delivered a brilliant speech on behalf of Sogo, charging that much of the prosecutor's evidence was distorted and that a conviction had been sought for political purposes.

In Japan as in the U.S., the wheels of justice grind slowly. The Appeals Court ruling was delivered April 24, 1929, nearly two years after Sogo had been convicted, more than three years after he was arrested and fired from his job. The verdict: Not guilty on all counts due to insufficient evidence. Ryohei Matsuhashi, the stock market trader, also was found not guilty. Kennosuke Inaba, the bureaucrat who had arranged for purchase of land after the earthquake, was found guilty and sentenced to 14 months in prison.

Sogo was feted at victory parties in Tokyo and Osaka attended by hundreds of friends. There was much toasting with cups of sake and many, many speeches. Sengoku said to loud applause: "This trial hit Sogo like a thunderbolt. It is said that a man who is hit by a thunderbolt and survives is assured of a long, long life. Sogo, you may have benefited from this sorry experience." At the Osaka party Oita delivered a moving speech about the courage and virtues of his friend Sogo that brought tears to the eyes of many.

Sogo noted wryly: "I was arrested and tried by politics. It was totally absurd." But his joy was dampened by Shinpei Goto's death from a stroke just 11 days before the Appeals Court ruling. "How sad," Sogo mourned, "that I could not tell him that his faith in me was vindicated."

Sogo was now 45 years old. He had no job and had not worked regularly for more than three years. Torao Oita's gifts and a little money picked up here and there had kept his family fed and clothed. He had worked briefly as an adviser to the Hanshin Electric Railway Company, where his greatest contribution was the introduction of speedy limited express trains that ran from Kobe to Kyoto with only one stop in Osaka. While riding the route he noticed that few passengers boarded or left the train at the numerous small stops. Quietly he filed a limited express application with the Railways Ministry and tied up the permit before competitors knew what was happening. Sogo might have had a bright future at Hanshin, but he resigned when the president was arrested on charges of bribery in connection with illegal currency trading.

Sogo also took a fling at producing educational motion pictures. Disgusted with what he was seeing on the screen, he got together with some technical people and started up a movie company. They had just completed a samurai epic depicting such virtues as courage and loyalty when a fire burned down the studio and destroyed the film.

Soon afterward Sogo received a telegram from Mitsugu Sengoku, who by then was president of Mantetsu, the South Manchuria Railway. Sengoku asked Sogo to accept an appointment as a director of Mantetsu.

Sogo was badly in need of a job. He admired Sengoku and knew he could work closely with his former boss. But he also had heard much disturbing information about Mantetsu. Without hesitation he declined the offer.

有法子

CHAPTER 9

CLOUDS OVER MANCHURIA

While Shinji Sogo was fighting to clear his name of politically motivated bribery charges, Japan itself was in a monumental struggle that would determine its national destiny. On the political right were ultra-nationalists, backed by the military establishment which had become increasingly disillusioned with the civilian-led government's desire to slash army and navy appropriations. In the center were business-oriented moderates and what were perceived to be "corrupt politicians," and on the left a dedicated but ineffective group of radicals.

The military officers, largely unsophisticated and unschooled in world affairs, considered themselves above politics but with a mandate to serve the Emperor and take responsibility for the nation's security and well-being. In practical terms, that meant an aggressive policy on the mainland where the Chinese had land and vast stores of natural resources, which Japan did not have, and stirring up political disorder that would make China easy prey for aggression. The strongest element on the right was the elite Kwantung Army, based in southern Manchuria to protect concessions acquired in 1905 under the Treaty of Portsmouth, which ended the Russo-Japanese War. The Kwantung Army held a curious semi-autonomous position, taking actions that at times seemed to be independent of civilian control from Tokyo.

The concessions included the Russian-built Chinese Eastern Railway's 260-mile route from Dalian on the coast across the flat Manchurian plain to Changchun in the heart of the province, with spur lines to the vast open-pit coal mines at Fushun and Yantai. Although Manchuria was a part of China, Japan was also authorized to station troops there to protect the railroad. To manage the railroad and mines, the South Manchuria Railway (Mantetsu) was established in November 1906. Half of the capital of ¥200 million was provided by the Japanese government and the other half by private investors and the Chinese government.

Mantetsu's first president was Shinpei Goto, who later was to play a major role in Shinji Sogo's life. By the 1920s Mantetsu was a profitable operation with express passenger service between Dalian and Changchun, but 90 percent of its business was hauling freight—coal, soybeans, soybean meal and oil, and other agricultural products and consumer goods from Japanese factories for the Manchurian market. Manchuria produced something like 4 million tons of soybeans annually, 60 percent of the world's supply. A large part of the output helped meet Japan's food needs. The meal went into livestock feed and fertilizer. By the 1930s Mantetsu headquarters in Dalian boasted hundreds of employees fluent in Chinese, Russian, and English, as well as Japanese, 600 typewriters, direct-dial telephones, and an IBM punchcard system for processing data. It was an efficient, modern operation.

Mantetsu's original mission was to run the railroad and port facilities and mine and ship coal to power Japanese industries. But Manchuria was undeveloped industrially, and it did not take long for Mantetsu's ambitious executives to expand their activities. Soon Mantetsu was the spearhead of Japan's economic penetration of Manchuria. At its peak, Mantetsu controlled or owned interests in some 80 major companies, including sugar refineries, cotton and wool spinning mills, glass manufacturing, timber production, fire insurance, hydroelectric power, a shipping line, construction and engineering firms, and many other enterprises. An uneasy cooperative relationship existed between Mantetsu and the Kwantung Army. While the army's primary responsibility was peacekeeping, it had its own ideas about how to develop Manchuria. The essence of its plan was to convert Manchuria into a base for an inevitable war with Russia for control of East Asia. That involved an influx of Japanese capital and Japanese settlers to diversify the economy rather than leave control in Mantetsu's hands. In fact, some Kwantung Army strategists entertained the possibility of attracting American investments in Manchuria.

But it was primarily assurance that Mantetsu would look after them that drew thousands of Japanese entrepreneurs to Manchuria. Thus Mantetsu executives, particularly its presidents, were men of considerable influence in Japanese business and politics.

In the spring of 1927 the Reijiro Wakatsuki cabinet resigned after the House of Peers turned down an emergency bill to provide additional funds to shore up Japan's official Bank of Taiwan.

Wakatsuki's successor as prime minister was Giichi Tanaka, a former army general who headed the Minseito Party. Two months after taking office Tanaka convened what was called the Orient Council. Its purpose was to formulate a long-range policy toward China which, under Generalissimo Chiang Kai-shek, was beginning to show signs of national unity. Summoned to the meeting were Japanese diplomats from various East Asian posts and top military officers, including representatives of the Kwantung Army.

While the meeting was called in the prime minister's name, the person obviously in charge was Kaku Mori, the 44-year-old vice foreign minister and Tanaka confidant. Mori was an up-and-coming young political leader whose name had appeared vaguely during Sogo's bribery trial as among those that the public prosecutor general wanted to embarrass. The new policy, which came to be known as the Tanaka Memorandum, arrived at on July 7, 1927, but never fully publicized, was clearly interventionist and considered a blueprint for military aggression. It said Japan would promote separation of Manchuria and Mongolia from China, and to protect its national interests, Japan would take responsibility for the security of the two regions. In other words, a political land-grab bound to cause some worried frowns, particularly since it appeared the Foreign Ministry was collaborating with the military in Washington, London, and Geneva, where the League of Nations was headquartered. But the threat was vague. Nothing was said as to when and how the policy would be implemented.

Nearly a year later the questions were partly answered. On the morning of June 4, 1928, General Zhang Zuolin, Manchuria's most powerful warlord who had been cooperating with the Japanese, was returning from Beijing (formerly Peking) in North China to Shenyang on a Mantetsu train when it was blown up. General Zhang and many of his staff were killed.

Shinji Sogo, "father of the Bullet Train," was a widely admired calligrapher. With ink brush he wrote his motto, *Youfazi*, a Chinese saying meaning "Nothing Is Impossible."

Sogo at 18, taken in 1902 after he was named class vice president at Saijo Middle School.

Sogo (far left) in 1903 with colleagues accepted by Ichiko School in Tokyo and by the Military Academy.

Students at Ueno Music Academy in Tokyo, about 1906. Kiku Okazaki, who became Sogo's wife, is second from the left.

Sogo at 24 and bride Kiku at 20. Taken in 1908, about a year after their marriage.

Typical classroom scene at Tokyo Imperial University, early 1900s.

The famous *Akamon*, or Red Gate, at Tokyo Imperial University.

Shortly before graduation in 1909, Sogo affected a beard and mustache.

Shinpei Goto (1857-1929), who persuaded Sogo to join the Railway Agency. He ordered Sogo to trim his facial hair.

Cover of a book on railway economics translated by Sogo from the original English.

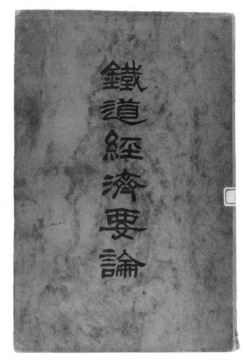

鐵道經濟要論

Sogo was called up for duty as a corporal in the paymaster's section in 1911. Sogo is fourth from the right.

Tokyo Station in 1914, shortly after it was completed. Much of the original structure is still in use. *Courtesy of the Transportation Museum, Tokyo.*

Sogo (center in the front row) with some of his Railway Agency colleagues, all in military-style railway uniforms.

Family photo taken in 1917 just before Sogo left for the U.S. Michiko (center) was 7. Kosaku (right) was 9.

Sogo (fourth from the left in the front row) with Saijo School students on the eve of his departure for America.

Genevieve Caulfield, blind
since birth, taught Sogo
English in New York. Later
she established a school for
the blind in Bangkok.
Photo was taken in Saigon.
Date unknown.

Portrait of Mrs. William
Diller Matthew in whose
home Sogo stayed in 1917.

After his return from the U.S., Sogo (far left) escorted an American engineer who introduced new construction machinery to Japan.

Postcard issued by the Railways Ministry in 1921, in observance of the 50th anniversary of railroads in Japan.

Torao Oita (1884-1948), Sogo's best friend, who shared his salary with Sogo's family during the years he was unemployed.

Mitsugu Sengoku (1857-1931), who persuaded Sogo to join him in managing the South Manchuria Railway.

Sogo, at 46, shortly after
he was appointed a director of
the South Manchuria Railway.

Inaugural photo of South Manchuria Railway's President Kosai Uchida (seated,
left) and Vice President Teijo Eguchi (seated, right). Director Sogo is third from
the right, standing.

Banquet for high-ranking officers of the Kwantung Army and South Manchuria Railway officials. In the front row, third from the left is Colonel Seishiro Itagaki, fourth from the left is General Nobuyoshi Muto, and next to him is Lieutenant General Shigeru Honjo. Sogo is in the back row, fifth from the left. Date unknown.

Geisha party in Dalian. At left in the front row is Colonel Seishiro Itagaki, with Sogo next to him. Probably August 1932.

Kaku Mori, a businessman and politician, was a good friend of Sogo's and an expert on China.

Family photo, 1932. Seated, from the left, are daughter Michiko, Sogo, and wife Kiku. Children in the front row are Keiko and Shinsaku. In the back row, fourth from the left, is son Kosaku, second from the right is Kazuhei, and far right is Rinzo.

About 1936. As president of Kochu Konsu, Sogo spoke often about the need for Sino-Japanese cooperation.

Sogo, next to his wife Kiku, took sons Shinsaku (center) and Rinzo (far right) on a pilgrimage to Minobu-san Temple in Shizuoka Prefecture in 1936.

Early in 1937, Sogo (right) was drafted to help General Senjuro Hayashi (left) organize a cabinet. Hayashi proved totally inept, and Sogo resigned shortly after this photo was taken.

The last family portrait of Sogo's first son, Kosaku, and his family: wife Miyoko, daughter Motoko, and son Kazumoto. Kosaku died when his ship was torpedoed in 1942.

Meeting of graduates of the elite Ichiko School, probably in the late 1940s. Sogo is seated, far left.

Near war's end in 1945, Sogo visited Saijo near his birthplace and was asked to accept appointment as mayor. Sogo (fourth from the left, standing) visited with city leaders.

The Kwantung Army, which was responsible for security, blamed Chiang Kai-shek's agents.

Actually, Colonel Daisaku Komoto of the Kwantung Army had masterminded the assassination. Zhang Zuolin was beginning to show a bit too much independence, and besides, a terrorist act by "bandits" against a presumed friend of Japan would give the Kwantung Army an excuse to crack down. It was not revealed until after World War II that an angry Emperor Hirohito had demanded that Colonel Komoto be punished. The Kwantung Army made it clear the generals did not want any action taken against Komoto, and Prime Minister Tanaka only suspended the colonel. Then, because he had failed to carry out the Emperor's request, Tanaka and his cabinet resigned on July 2, 1929. (The relationship between Mantetsu and the Kwantung Army can be seen in the fact that Colonel Komoto later became a Mantetsu director. At the end of World War II he was captured by Chinese Communist troops, jailed as a war criminal, and died behind bars in 1953 at age 70.)

Tanaka's successor as prime minister, Yuko Hamaguchi, took a much more moderate stance toward China. He appointed Kijuro Shidehara, who wanted to respect China's sovereignty and stay out of Chinese internal affairs, as foreign minister. He also asked Mitsugu Sengoku, who supported Shidehara's policy, to take over as president of Mantetsu. Sengoku knew that Mantetsu was having financial problems. A competing railroad built by the Chiang Kai-shek government was proving to be a heavy drain on Mantetsu profits. In addition, Japan was feeling the effects of the Black Thursday American stock market crash on October 24, 1929. The financial impact sped around the world in a way that most Americans, with their insular point of view, could not understand. In Japan, factories shut down and unemployment spread. The government stepped up its efforts to send impoverished citizens to Manchuria where there would be jobs and enough to eat. Meanwhile, investments in Manchuria by Japan's huge industrial conglomerates tailed off. It was obvious to Sengoku there would be big problems ahead. He was 72 years old, had been drinking excessively for years, and was a diabetic. Nonetheless, he felt it a duty to accept the Mantetsu assignment. One of his first acts was to replace the directors with men he knew and could trust, among them Sogo.

In at first declining the offer, Sogo told Sengoku he knew Mantetsu employees wanted to see one of their own promoted rather than an outsider, adding that Mantetsu executives should have enough commitment to die for their employer, but that he wasn't quite ready for that.

Almost in desperation, Sengoku asked Torao Oita to persuade his friend to accept the appointment. Sogo finally agreed to take the position on two conditions.

"First," Sogo told Sengoku, "I will work for Mantetsu only so long as you are president. When you leave, I also leave.

"Second," said Sogo, recognizing Sengoku's health problems, "you must agree to let me bring you back home to Japan when you are no longer able to serve the nation."

If Sengoku thought Sogo insolent, he said nothing. Sogo was appointed a director of Mantetsu on July 11, 1930. Among those who congratulated him was Minister of Railways Tasuku Egi, who had been justice minister when Sogo was brought to trial. In September Sogo and Sengoku sailed for Dalian. At the wharf in Dalian was a banner saying "Corrupt Directors Not Wanted." It was in reference to Sogo's bribery trial and had been put up by the right-leaning Manchuria Youth Association with a membership of some 5,000 Japanese, many of them employed by Mantetsu. It was not a reassuring welcome for Sogo.

Despite the variety and complexity of the issues Sogo faced, his first knotty problem was almost ridiculous. Mantetsu was erecting a statue to honor its first president, Shinpei Goto. The unveiling was set for April 29, 1931, and President Sengoku was to make the dedicatory address. But Sengoku disliked Goto intensely and could not bring himself to say anything laudatory about his predecessor even though he was deceased.

"I know so many bad things about Goto but not one good thing," Sengoku complained to Sogo. Nonetheless, Sogo who had been one of Goto's protégés, was assigned to draft a speech for Sengoku to deliver. Sengoku's reaction was predictable. "This part is too flattering," he grumbled. "This part is a lie." Sogo had to grit his teeth and edit the draft to Sengoku's satisfaction. Said Sogo of his boss: "He gave his complete love and support to people he trusted, but hated those he did not. He could never accept compromise. Sengoku was aligned with the Mitsubishi interests. Goto was on the side of Mitsui, the powerful rival conglomerate. That may have been one main reason for their hostility."

"I learned a lot from Shinpei Goto when I was young, and I learned a lot from Sengoku later in my career," Sogo once said. "These two great men were my mentors as well as my teachers. Their enmity put me in a very difficult position."

As it turned out, Goto's statue, depicting him impressively in a morning coat, was dedicated in a ceremony attended by a large throng of Mantetsu employees and even school children. Sengoku read his speech which, if not excessively laudatory, seemed to satisfy Goto's friends and relatives.

Sogo's next mission for Sengoku was considerably more substantial. He was summoned to Sengoku's office one day when the old man seemed to be more whimsical than usual.

"The stupid minister of railways has come up with a stupid idea," Sengoku said. "As part of the 'Buy Japanese' campaign, he's saying the Railways Ministry is cutting in half its purchases of Manchurian coal from the Fushun mine because it's a 'foreign product.' Everybody knows Japan made Fushun coal a Japanese product at a cost of 100,000 lives and ¥2 billion, even though the deposit is in Manchuria. Go tell Minister Egi we aren't going to sell him a single ton of coal unless he faces the facts." Sogo picked up the cue and went to Tokyo to meet Egi. After the usual pleasantries the conversation went like this:

Sogo: "Mr. Minister, I have discovered that in the world there are many fools."

Egi: "Yes? What sort of fools are they?"

Sogo: "I have heard there is a fool who says Japan should not use Fushun coal because it is a foreign product, and everyone knows it has become a Japanese product through great sacrifice. Isn't that amazing?"

Egi smiled, and no more was said. After some idle conversation Sogo left. He went directly to the Railways Ministry's purchasing office and asked the chief to prepare two purchase orders, each for 1.5 million tons of Fushun coal, and then take them in for Egi's signature and seal. He hoped that if he could not get an order for 3 million tons, Egi would approve half that amount.

Egi was still smiling when he signed both contracts. Sogo stopped overnight at a hotel in Shimonoseki, where he was scheduled to board a ship for Dalian, when he was called on by a group of Kyushu miners demanding reduction of Fushun coal imports. When it seemed they would not accept the argument that Manchurian coal was domestic coal, Sogo took an opposite tack. He pointed out that Japan's resources were extremely limited and it made sense for the nation to buy cheap mainland coal during the recession and conserve domestic coal for some future time. The miners may not have understood Sogo's argument, but it quieted them down.

Sogo obviously was a persuasive talker. On the same trip he persuaded the Mitsui interests, which marketed domestic coal as well as Fushun coal under an exclusive sales contract, to agree to let other companies share in distributing the Manchurian product.

"What Mitsui can sell of our coal is not enough to keep Mantetsu going," Sogo explained to Baron Takuma Dan, chief of the Mitsui conglomerate. "But if you can see your way to help us increase the market, it will help Mantetsu regain its vigor and fight off the Chinese strategy of a competitive railroad to bankrupt us."

Baron Dan could see the logic of Sogo's appeal to patriotism. "How can Mitsui deny a reasonable request?" he asked. "We will do as you wish starting tomorrow. But say nothing to anyone in the Mitsui organization. If we handle this poorly, there is bound to be opposition. I will take care of the matter."

But Sogo's coup was not greeted happily in high Mantetsu circles where many had links with Mitsui. Knowing of Sengoku's Mitsubishi affiliations, some Mantetsu officials suspected the open contract was a trick to undercut Mitsui. The controversy was quieted only when Sengoku announced Mitsui's exclusive contract was canceled. (A year later Baron Dan was assassinated by a rightist gunman in front of the Mitsui Bank Building in Tokyo.)

Sengoku's tenure as Mantetsu president was short. In November of 1930, Prime Minister Yuko Hamaguchi was shot and seriously wounded by another rightist terrorist. Sengoku went to see him in Tokyo and fell seriously ill on the trip. He seemed to recover, but Sogo could see his physical and mental powers had deteriorated substantially. Sogo's mother, So-u, died in May of 1931 at age 76. During the time he was in Japan for the funeral, Sogo met with government leaders and urged them to persuade Sengoku to resign. The following month Sengoku agreed to retire. Kosai Uchida, a four-time foreign minister, was chosen as his successor, and Teijo Eguchi, a Mitsubishi official, became vice president.

When Sengoku left office Sogo, as per his agreement, also turned in his resignation. The new president, Uchida, refused to accept it, and Sengoku, who was bedridden by then, urged Sogo to change his mind. Sogo was uncomfortable with the way the Kwantung Army seemed to be setting Japan's Manchuria policy. His experience in the United States convinced him that some day there might be a confrontation with his country over aggression on the mainland. He had no idea what he might do to steer Japan on a more moderate course. He also knew that the entire Japanese economy depended heavily on Manchuria, and the Kwantung Army had a very large say in Japan-China relations. Perhaps by continuing to work with Mantetsu, he would be able to help steer a course that would be beneficial to Japan. In the end he agreed to stay with Mantetsu.

Every day that he was in Tokyo, Sogo visited the dying Sengoku. One day Mrs. Sengoku told Sogo that she had gone to the Mitsubishi Bank to make her usual cash withdrawal. A bank official returned her request, explaining that they were authorized to loan Sengoku up to ¥1 million, but now the debt exceeded ¥1.5 million. Mrs. Sengoku said she was told she would have to make further arrangements before she could be advanced any more cash.

"What shall I do?" Mrs. Sengoku asked Sogo. "I have never worried about money, and I have no idea how much my husband has." Sogo took her problem to the head of the Mitsubishi conglomerate. He was told not to worry, Mitsubishi would take care of Mrs. Sengoku's problem.

Sogo came away very much aware of his own precarious financial position, and of the way big business took care of its own.

有法子

CHAPTER 10

WAR COMES TO MANCHURIA

About midnight on September 18, 1931, the telephone rang in Shinji Sogo's room at the Yamato Hotel in Dalian. Grumbling sleepily, Sogo answered. It was Mantetsu headquarters reporting that fighting had broken out between Kwantung Army units and Chinese forces along the railroad near Shenyang.

For weeks during the summer there had been a series of hostile events involving Chinese and Japanese and growing rumors that something serious was in the air. "So the attack has come," Sogo said to himself. Shenyang was hours away by rail, the fastest mode of transportation. For safety reasons, no trains ran at night. There was nothing he could do. After making sure other high Mantetsu officials were notified, Sogo went back to bed.

In July there had been an outbreak of violence in a remote area of southern Manchuria near Wanpaoshan. Korean immigrants, who had rented farmland in the area under Japanese protection, were attacked by Chinese farmers. Inflammatory press reports stirred Korean anger and touched off violence against Chinese residents in Korea. More than 100 were killed and 160 injured. About the same time Captain Shintaro Nakamura of the Kwantung Army was seized by Chinese troops in northern Manchuria and executed. Nakamura was reportedly on an inspection tour, but the Chinese contended he was on an espionage mission. In Tokyo the War Ministry declared Nakamura's execution was a clear sign of Chinese aggression against Japan and pressured the Foreign Ministry to demand punishment.

The government was in a difficult position. At times the Kwantung Army seemed to be setting policy for the government in Manchuria in defiance of Tokyo. The War Ministry itself was divided between younger firebrands who sided with the Kwantung Army and older and more conservative generals. On August 1, 1931, Lieutenant General Shigeru Honjo was assigned command of the Kwantung Army. He arrived at headquarters in Shenyang on August 20. On September 18, units of the Kwantung Army were on night maneuvers near Shenyang when an explosion blew up a section of the Mantetsu line. There was little doubt it had been touched off by Japanese troops. The Kwantung Army maneuvers quickly became a full-fledged assault against a Chinese garrison nearby. Before morning the Kwantung Army was in control of Shenyang. Other units of the Kwantung Army obviously hadn't been asleep that night. Moving in accord, they seized cities like Andong, Yingkou, and Changchun, and Chinese troops withdrew to the countryside.

For several days prior to September 18, there had been a flurry of meetings in occupied areas. More than 40 years later it was revealed that on September 14 a Kwantung Army officer in the Fushun area had told Japanese civilian officials that his troops soon would seize a Chinese airport nearby. He had asked Mantetsu to provide rail transportation in support of that operation. Mantetsu telegraphed the information to its Tokyo headquarters, which then warned the Foreign Ministry. Another version has it that the consulate general in Shenyang notified the Foreign Ministry that something was up. In any event, an emergency cabinet meeting was held September 15 in Tokyo. Foreign Minister Shidehara accused War Minister Minami of plotting an incident. Minami denied complicity but admitted suspicion that some young colonels in the Kwantung Army might be acting on their own. Lieutenant General Yoshitsugu Tatekawa was dispatched to Kwantung Army headquarters with orders to bring about some discipline. Shortly afterward Colonel Seishiro Itagaki at Kwantung Army headquarters received a telegram from a colonel in Tokyo headquarters. Reportedly, it said: "Information leaked. Tatekawa is on his way. Do it before he gets there."

The "it" referred to concerted attacks against Chinese troops which had been planned for September 28. Colonel Itagaki and his co-plotter, Colonel Kanji Ishiwara, were confident they could persuade General Tatekawa that it was necessary to bring all of Manchuria under Japanese control, and attacking Chinese troops was the way to do it. But if General Tatekawa were bringing a direct order from Emperor Hirohito prohibiting the attack, that would be a different story. So it was decided to strike on September 18, before Tatekawa arrived.

Within Mantetsu there was as much confusion as in the Japanese government itself. Most rank-and-file employees were strongly in support of the Kwantung Army. Said one: "We are different from the highly paid executives who come to Mantetsu temporarily from other government agencies. Their concern about what happens in Manchuria is shallow. After a time they will go back to other jobs in Japan. We live here. We make our livelihoods here and serve our country under dangerous conditions. The Kwantung Army protects us from the Chinese bandits so that we can go on with the work of running the railroad. We should support the army."

After the shooting ended at Shenyang, many Mantetsu workers in Dalian left their jobs and took the train, as though on a picnic, to see what had happened. Giddy over the triumph of Japanese forces, they were anxious to cooperate with the army in any way. On September 22, Mantetsu President Uchida was notified by the Ministry of Foreign Affairs that the government had no intention of expanding hostilities in Manchuria, that every effort would be made to solve problems through diplomacy, and that Mantetsu was not to become involved in military activities other than at the request of the War, Foreign, and Overseas Affairs ministries. There could be no doubt: What the Kwantung Army was up to was not government policy, and Mantetsu was not to give it any assistance.

When Mantetsu directors convened to discuss the situation, it was immediately obvious the overwhelming majority was loyal to the Tokyo government. One of the few who spoke out for supporting the Kwantung Army was Shinji Sogo.

This was a sharp reversal of Sogo's position. What had caused him to change his mind? Sogo said that, as a result of its own actions, the Kwantung Army had created trouble for itself. But without Kwantung Army support, Mantetsu and Japan itself were in trouble. Therefore, like it or not, Mantetsu had no option but to support the Kwantung Army. There was nodding around the table, but no decision was reached. After the meeting, one of the directors asked Sogo to sign a directive that said: "All Mantetsu directors should act only within the areas of responsibility assigned to them and avoid interfering in matters outside their responsibility." Sogo signed it and then asked the director, "Have you ever served in the military?"

The director said he had not. Then Sogo said: "I have. The military has regulations which are observed very strictly in times of peace. However, the regulations permit soldiers to exercise their judgment during war. Exceptions to the regulations are permitted in emergencies. This should also be true at Mantetsu. Tell the president what I have told you."

A few days later President Uchida and Vice President Eguchi were ordered back to Tokyo for conferences. Sogo asked what would be discussed. "I have been asked for a firsthand report on the situation in Manchuria, and to mediate disagreements between the Foreign Ministry and War Ministry," Uchida said.

Sogo responded: "Sir, if I may say so, you have never had an opportunity to meet with the senior officers of the Kwantung Army. It would seem very difficult for you to act as mediator without knowing what they are thinking. In Shenyang, the Kwantung Army, the Foreign Ministry represented by the consul general, and Mantetsu have different opinions, and they are not communicating. It might be unwise, if not dangerous, for you to go to Tokyo without knowing what is being said. May I suggest that you postpone your trip back to Japan until you can meet with them?"

Uchida replied that it was urgent that he go to Tokyo, and there just wasn't time to meet the generals in Shenyang.

"What do you plan to propose to Tokyo?" Sogo persisted. Uchida admitted he had no plan.

"You would be prudent to have some ideas," Sogo said. "If you are to mediate successfully, you need to know what the generals are thinking."

After a pause, Uchida said: "All right. Make arrangements for me to see General Honjo as soon as possible."

The atmosphere at Kwantung Army headquarters in Shenyang was extremely hostile toward Mantetsu. The consensus seemed to be that Mantetsu was being run by a bunch of cowardly fools. "Who do they think this war is for?" one officer asked. "Since we are fighting for them, the least they can do is to supply us with funds and transportation."

Sogo met with Colonel Itagaki and set the Uchida-Honjo conference for October 6 in Shenyang. The two top officials held an hour-long, private session beginning at 2 p.m. Then senior Kwantung Army officers and Mantetsu senior directors joined them. Afterward Uchida told Sogo: "It was a good meeting. I have made up my mind." That evening Uchida hosted a dinner for Kwantung Army officers at the Yamato Hotel.

During the banquet Uchida made a speech. In essence, he said that what was being called the Manchurian Incident had passed the crisis stage. Manchuria, he continued, now should be dealt with not as a problem between Japan and China, but as part of a global problem. And Mantetsu should do all it can to cooperate with the Kwantung Army in reaching an equitable solution. In effect, he was endorsing the Kwantung Army's aggression.

Aside from General Honjo's people, there was no one at the banquet, or later at a meeting for Mantetsu employees in Dalian, who was not surprised by Uchida's position. It was a 180-degree change from what Mantetsu's Vice President Eguchi had been saying to all the Japanese civilians in Manchuria.

In pursuit of a joint effort, the Kwantung Army next day presented Mantetsu with a sweeping outline of its objectives. It set as a goal the political separation of Manchuria and Mongolia from China with local Chinese—puppets—governing the two provinces under Japanese direction. The implication was that this would be accomplished by force, if necessary. It called for Mantetsu to extend its rail lines into these areas, establish air routes, and create a new agency to promote the economy. When President Uchida left Shenyang on his way to Japan, all senior officers of the Kwantung Army—including General Honjo— were at the station to pay him the honor of seeing him off.

Uchida took the train down through the Korean Peninsula to Pusan, where he boarded a ship for the overnight trip to the closest Japanese port, Shimonoseki. Vice President Eguchi was to join him there for the long rail journey to Tokyo. But Eguchi's ship from Dalian was delayed by bad weather, and Uchida went on ahead to Kyoto where he called on Prince Kinmochi Saionji, a still-powerful elder statesman, to report on developments. Such a report, in the absence of dissent from Saionji, was tantamount to government acceptance of policy. There could not be a reversal without a devastating political crisis.

By some accounts, Uchida's meeting with Saionji had been neither authorized nor scheduled. Vice President Eguchi was stunned when he heard that Uchida had come out in support of the Kwantung Army and outraged that he had seen Saionji on his own. When Eguchi caught up with Uchida, they engaged in a heated argument at their hotel in Kyoto. Clearly, their views were incompatible. Within months Eguchi was fired. But Uchida, too, left Mantetsu shortly, as continuing turmoil created cabinet changes.

If Eguchi was stunned by Uchida's actions, Foreign Minister Shidehara was furious. He thought he had explained the government's position clearly to Uchida during their telephone conferences, and he thought he had Uchida's promise of support. When he visited the dying Sengoku, Sogo's previous boss at Mantetsu, Shidehara denounced Sogo as a pawn of the militarists and blamed him for Uchida's change of heart.

Some time later, after Sengoku's death, Sogo called on his widow who was seriously ill. Holding his hand, she told him: "Mr. Sogo, I cannot die before I carry out a duty. Mr. Sengoku knew what you really were up to at the start of the Manchurian Incident. He knew very well that you acted as you did, not because you are a militarist but because you cared about our country. I must convince Mr. Shidehara of this. Otherwise, I cannot face my husband in the other world when I die."

Meanwhile, Sogo was working to utilize the stability brought about by Kwantung Army aggression to establish a new nation in Manchuria separated from the chaos of China. He envisioned a democratic country based on "the rule of right," in which five ethnic groups could live in peace and prosperity. The five were the Ching (Manchus), Han (Chinese), Mongols, Koreans, and Japanese. He analyzed the Kwantung Army leadership as being divided between realists, who wanted to expand Japanese influence on the mainland by any means, and idealists, who saw the use of force as a necessary but temporary approach to creating a peaceful society in East Asia.

As a stopgap measure for governing Manchuria, the Kwantung Army set up a civilian administration and asked Mantetsu to provide the specialists needed to make it work. Sogo refused to cooperate, because it looked like an occupation agency. The Kwantung Army then proposed a board called the Northeast Transportation Committee to oversee reconstruction, with Sogo as chief adviser and a staff made up largely of Mantetsu personnel. This was more to Sogo's liking. The heads of various Chinese railway companies in Manchuria agreed to become members of the committee, but ultimate power was vested in Sogo, by then a seasoned, 47-year-old bureaucrat.

Before the committee could be organized, Sogo was stricken with typhoid fever. Since typhoid was contagious and in view of Sogo's key role, the nature of his illness was not announced. His wife Kiku received a telegram instructing her to come to Manchuria as quickly as possible. Because of the frequency of political assassinations in Tokyo as well as Manchuria, it was feared for a time that Sogo had been shot. The typhoid attack proved to be less serious than it had appeared, but Sogo was transferred to a hospital in Kobe to complete his recovery.

While he was hospitalized, the latest commander of the Kwantung Army asked Mantetsu to come up with a comprehensive blueprint for the economic development of Manchuria and Mongolia. Mantetsu executives agreed to sponsor what would be called the Economic Research Committee. Now the question was who would head it. A number of names were proposed, but Sogo, partly because of the credibility he had in Kwantung Army circles, was the only person everyone could agree upon.

Sogo liked the idea of the study because it seemed to address the very sort of course he envisioned for Manchuria. But he had some basic concerns that needed to be addressed.

"The area for study covers all of Manchuria and not just those portions where Mantetsu is involved," he said. "Thus, the committee's activities will extend beyond Mantetsu authority, and the head of the committee will have greater power than a Mantetsu director. As a Mantetsu director, I cannot assume that kind of responsibility. On the other hand, if I should yield to your insistence that I take the position, I should resign as a Mantetsu director."

Mantetsu did not want to lose his services. At the same time it was obvious there was no one better suited to head the committee. In the end Mantetsu's board agreed that Sogo would remain a director, but as head of the Economic Research Committee, he would have the independence to reach decisions unfavorable to Mantetsu and might even give orders to the president. The committee would report directly to the president of

Mantetsu, while at the same time it would function as a totally independent organization. Sogo referred to the body as the Economic Research Committee of Manchuria, not of Mantetsu. It was, Sogo observed dryly, a planning effort with unprecedented powers.

Nonetheless, Sogo anticipated a less hectic period of his life. He moved part of his family into a Mantetsu company house for executives in an exclusive part of Dalian. Kosaku, the eldest son, took up residence in a YMCA dormitory in Kyoto until his graduation from Kyoto Imperial University in April, when he was scheduled to join the Mitsubishi Corporation. Daughter Michiko was betrothed to Yukio Kagayama, a graduate in law from Tokyo Imperial University who had joined the Ministry of Railways. Son Rinzo, 16, went to live with his mother's parents while finishing junior high school studies. Son Kazuhei, 12, lived with an uncle and went to elementary school in Tokyo. Kiku, and six-year-old Keiko and three-year-old Shinsaku settled down in Dalian.

This must have been Kiku's most comfortable, if not happiest, time of life. She had more freedom than in Japan for social activities, and household chores were taken care of by Chinese servants. Their home, with a splendid ocean view, had central heating. Best of all, although Shinji seemed to be busier than ever, he could come home nights.

But not every night. As was expected of a man of his stature, Sogo had taken a geisha as his mistress. He would dine with her on occasion, pass the evening drinking and talking, use her as a sounding board for his ideas, and finally spend the night with her. There was little doubt that Kiku was aware of the relationship, but she accepted it as natural. Sogo, for his part, was discrete. Few knew he had a mistress, and some expressed surprise that he didn't seem to have one, as many prominent men did. Only when Sogo and his mistress were in an automobile accident did their relationship become widely known.

Sogo took over chairmanship of the Economic Research Committee in January of 1932. He chose as his vice chairman Tetsuo Ishikawa, a Mantetsu research director and former German-language teacher who also had attended Ichiko High School. Sections on planning, mining and industry, transportation, commerce and agriculture, laws and diplomacy, and a secretariat were established. It is significant that the Kwantung Army had a seat on the board.

The committee's intentions were good, but from the beginning, prospects for its effectiveness were not. Almost as soon as Sogo took over, another "incident" took place near Shanghai. Protesting an "illegal" Chinese boycott, the Japanese landed 70,000 troops and launched an attack on the Chinese 19th Route Army, which was based not far from the International Settlement. It was May before an agreement was reached. Hundreds of miles to the north, the new state of Manchoukuo was proclaimed on March 1. This should have been good news for Sogo's committee, but it quickly became evident that its ties with the government were tenuous at best, and implementation of the committee's plans was totally dependent on the support of the Kwantung Army. While key posts in the Manchoukuo government were held by Chinese and Manchus, and Henry Pu-yi, son of the last Empress of China, was installed as Emperor, Japanese behind the scenes had the real power. In fact, at one point Shinji Sogo was proposed for prime minister of Manchoukuo, a suggestion he quickly discouraged.

Even among the Japanese there was much confusion as to how Manchoukuo should be governed. Some among the millions of Japanese civilians in the country proposed setting up a government through responsible political parties, the way it was done back home. A few months after the founding of Manchoukuo, a political party called Kyowa-kai was established. The character for *kyo* in Kyowa means "cooperation," indicating the group's goal of unity among ethnic groups. But the first part of *Kyosan-to*, the word for Communist party, has the same sound.

Even such an innocent coincidence was enough to upset the generals to whom communism was anathema. As a matter of fact, there were elements among the Japanese in Manchoukuo who believed a controlled economy such as in the Soviet Union was not a bad idea for a new country heavily dependent on agriculture. And there were not a few army officers who believed Japanese troops should withdraw from the country once it became well-established, a proposal included in the Lytton Commission report to the League of Nations.

In fact, the Japanese army itself was badly divided. Three months after the founding of Manchoukuo, military reactionaries in Tokyo assassinated Prime Minister Tsuyoshi Inukai. The traditional political parties admitted their inability to run the country, and a nonparty cabinet was installed under Viscount Makoto Saito. His war minister was General Sadao Araki who quickly launched a major reorganization of the Kwantung Army's command structure.

Sogo was distressed to see many of his friends, who supported his Economic Research Committee, being transferred. General Nobuyoshi Muto, one rank above Lieutenant General Honjo, became Japan's top military man in Manchoukuo with the concurrent rank of ambassador at large. Lieutenant General Kuniaki Koiso became the new military commander. One of his duties was to keep his eye on the Economic Research Committee.

Sogo found his relations with the new commanders growing progressively less cordial. On a trip to Tokyo he asked War Minister Sadao Araki whether he regarded the Manchurian Incident as an ordinary military action. Araki replied that he did.

"Then," Sogo asked, "why have you transferred so many of the officers who participated? The reshuffling of personnel gives the world the impression that the War Ministry does not regard the Kwantung Army's actions as normal military activity."

General Araki's flustered response did not satisfy Sogo. He left wondering what the future held for Mantetsu, his committee's study, and the status of Manchoukuo. Despite its violent birth, he envisioned Manchoukuo eventually becoming an independent nation under Japanese tutelage, cooperating with Japan for the mutual economic benefit of the people of both countries. The new military regime, under generals Muto and Koiso, viewed Manchoukuo as a colony of Japan, under quasi-military rule like Taiwan and Korea, and Sogo feared Japan's political and business establishment endorsed that course.

Early in 1933 the Kwantung Army was on the move again. It drove south and west from Manchuria, occupied the province of Jehol, and advanced south of the Great Wall into North China. About the same time the army submitted a proposal to Mantetsu separating it into two divisions—railways and industrial development. The obvious intent was to reduce Mantetsu's influence in Manchoukuo and place it under the military's supervision as it proceeded with its expansionist policy.

Greatly disturbed, Sogo led Mantetsu's fight to retain its independence. So vigorous was his campaign that the Tokyo cabinet, which had approved the separation plan, withdrew it. For the moment Sogo had triumphed, but he could see the handwriting on the wall. The Economic Research Committee, which he had directed with such high hopes, could point to minimal accomplishments in a little more than two years. He resigned as chairman in October of 1934 and returned as a director of Mantetsu. The committee itself was dissolved in September of 1936.

While the Economic Research Committee had not succeeded, Sogo still fostered dreams of cooperation between
Japanese and Chinese to develop East Asia. In his travels
through Central and South China on Mantetsu and Research
Committee business, he met many influential and wealthy
Chinese who supported his views. He had long discussions with
some of them, and one of the ideas that was born of these talks
was a joint Sino-Japanese bank to fund development projects.

The first step to starting such a venture was for Japan to
cease its aggression on the mainland, after which China would
call off its boycott of Japanese products. If that could be done,
and it was a big "if," Sogo learned there was plenty of money.
Some 10 million Chinese immigrants living in Southeast Asia
were sending millions of dollars a year to families and relatives
back home through the British Hong Kong-Shanghai Bank.
Oversea, Chinese businessmen were remitting as much as $300
million a year to China through the same bank to maintain a
balance of foreign exchange. But the bank wasn't doing much
about helping the Chinese finance development projects.

Why not found a bank to help meet China's needs?

有法子

CHAPTER 11

TURMOIL

It is difficult to understand how, in the face of continued reckless Japanese military aggression on the Asian mainland, Shinji Sogo could maintain his almost childlike faith that Japan and China could work together to develop the economy of East Asia and improve the living standards of its people. China's needs were vast and obvious, and there was a great opportunity for the Japanese people to help. But the will was missing. Japan was in the grip of a military clique that had little compassion. Sogo was well aware of the power and influence wielded by the Kwantung Army in Manchuria, its commitment to expansion regardless of cost, and the weakness of civilian leadership in Tokyo. This was not a combination likely to bring about a moderate policy.

Nonetheless, in the early summer of 1934 Sogo took his idea for a joint Sino-Japanese investment bank to the new cabinet headed by Prime Minister Keisuke Okada, a genial former admiral who had succeeded the short-lived Saito administration. Sogo suggested the bank should be capitalized at ¥100 million. He said he had been assured by Chinese friends that they would underwrite half the sum, and the other half would have to come from Japanese sources.

Prime Minister Okada thought it was a good idea. But Minister of Finance Korekiyo Takahashi vehemently opposed the bank. Great Britain will never tolerate an official Japanese challenge to the Hong Kong-Shanghai Bank's dominance in East Asia, he explained. Japan is having enough trouble with the West over Manchuria and cannot afford to antagonize the financially powerful British any further, he argued. Sogo's plan suffered a swift death from lack of support.

Four years had passed since Sogo had become a Mantetsu director. In that time Manchuria had been separated from China by military force and reorganized as a puppet of Japan. So long as rambunctious Japanese troops remained on the mainland, North China was a tinderbox that could burst into flames at any moment. Japan's domestic politics were in turmoil. Much of what Sogo had hoped to accomplish when he accompanied Mitsugu Sengoku into Mantetsu's management had not been realized, and under the circumstances there was little hope of success. Sogo felt it was time for change. He resigned from Mantetsu on July 10, 1934, without knowing where he would go or what he would do.

On retirement Sogo was entitled to an immediate lump sum payment plus a pension that would be paid out over a period of time. In view of the senior position he had held, neither amount was insignificant. When he returned to Japan he visited his old friend Torao Oita, who was living quietly at his ancestral home in the provinces. Bowing low, Sogo gave his entire lump sum payment to Oita in appreciation for the support his family had received during the bribery trial and the period of unemployment after that. Oita had no personal wealth. While working he had given much of his income to help others, and now he was in need. He wept as he accepted the money.

Sogo was now 50 years old, but too young and too full of ideas to remain inactive. He was still enthusiastic about a Sino-Japanese development bank, but if that proposal could stir little enthusiasm, he had another idea with similar objectives. Sogo reasoned that since a government-backed development bank was impractical, why not a privately operated joint venture to do essentially the same work? The organization was to be called Kochu Konsu (China Development Company). Its purpose would be to extract and market China's coal and iron ore, build electric generating plants, open textile mills, mine and export salt, develop railroads, and undertake other major projects—the same kinds of economic development activity Mantetsu had undertaken in Manchuria. Finance Minister Takahashi, who had blocked Sogo's first idea, was enthusiastic about the new proposal. He urged Sogo to accept the presidency of Kochu Konsu and make it work.

Sogo had little doubt that the idea was feasible, given the right conditions. But he had grown cautious from previous failures, and he voiced a number of reservations in a meeting early in 1935 with representatives of the army and Mantetsu whose financial support was essential.

They reached agreement to Sogo's satisfaction on four points: Mantetsu would provide ¥30 million to get Kochu Konsu started and would pledge additional capital; Mantetsu would be the sole Japanese investor; Mantetsu's administrative resources would be made available to Kochu Konsu, but Mantetsu would not interfere in the company's operations; the military would not interfere with Kochu Konsu, and the company would be free to cooperate with European and American interests.

It was expected Sogo would be named president of Kochu Konsu, but no action was taken pending the installation of Yosuke Matsuoka as president of Mantetsu on August 2, 1935. Matsuoka, who had studied at the University of Oregon, had been a Mantetsu vice president from 1927 to 1929 and was considered an expert on Chinese affairs. He also had the reputation of being a manipulator. Sogo and Matsuoka did not like each other. As it turned out, Matsuoka's presidency was short-lived. He was soon summoned back to Japan to serve as foreign minister in Prime Minister Koki Hirota's military-dominated cabinet. On November 25, 1936, Matsuoka signed the German-Japanese Anti-Comintern Pact directed against the Soviet Union. A similar Italian-Japanese treaty soon followed, setting up the Tri-Partite Axis alliance which ultimately led to the outbreak of World War II. But all that was in the future as Sogo waited to see how Matsuoka, as the new president, would react to Mantetsu's commitment to Kochu Konsu.

They met in September of 1935, with Sogo taking along several associates to make sure there would be witnesses to the discussions. The first day was a disaster. Matsuoka knew that Sogo would have to be named to head Kochu Konsu if it were to succeed, but he went out of his way to make the meeting unpleasant. At the same time Sogo, being equally difficult, insisted he was not qualified to take the job and rebuffed Matsuoka at every turn.

On the second day Sogo finally agreed to take the presidency. Matsuoka committed Mantetsu to invest ¥1 billion over a period of years and ¥10 million to get Kochu Konsu under way. Sogo requested a memorandum of the agreement, which

Matsuoka drafted and signed. After the meeting Matsuoka through an intermediary asked for return of the agreement. "This memorandum," he explained, "may give the impression that the great Mantetsu is controlled by a subsidiary company, and that would cause me to lose face. I will fulfill the terms, but please return the document to me."

Sogo didn't think there would be a problem with such a far-reaching agreement reached before witnesses and, in this era before copying machines, returned the document. Before long Sogo realized his error. He had to stand by helplessly while Matsuoka reduced Mantetsu's initial investment from ¥10 million to ¥2.5 million and tried to influence selection of the board of directors.

The new organization's inaugural ceremony was held on December 10, 1935, in Mantetsu's board room in Dalian. Kochu Konsu's headquarters were set up in rented space in Dalian, and branch offices were opened in Tianjin, Shanghai, Beijing, and Guangzhou. Sogo issued a directive to all employees that said:

"The purpose of Kochu Konsu is to build bridges between China and Japan through economic activities in China. All employees are urged to deepen their understanding of China and maintain good relations with the Chinese people. Our goal is not just to make profits, but to make as many Chinese friends as possible. The Chinese must not be exploited. If you have failed to make good friends among the Chinese in a year or two, you are not the kind of employee we want."

Several key executives from Mantetsu were transferred to Kochu Konsu. To give the organization credibility in Japan, Sogo named advisers from the Sumitomo conglomerate, Osaka Steamship Line, Mitsubishi, Mitsui, and Japan Industrial Bank. But these were uncertain times, and Sogo found progress difficult.

Two and a half months after the founding of Kochu Konsu,

a group of rebellious young military officers attempted a coup in Tokyo. This was the notorious Two-two-six Uprising of February 26, 1936, when Viscount Saito, Finance Minister Takahashi, and a number of other top government officials were assassinated in a coordinated early-morning attack, carried out in the name of the Emperor to restore military domination over a corrupt civilian government. But key senior generals remained loyal to the government, and the revolt failed. Seventeen of the rebel leaders were executed. Koki Hirota became prime minister of a cabinet dominated by the military, and the arms budget was boosted to placate the services.

Under such circumstances, Kochu Konsu was virtually helpless. While it struggled to survive, Japanese troops—again on night maneuvers—clashed with Chinese soldiers at Marco Polo Bridge near Beijing on July 7, 1937. It was a familiar scenario—dubious charges of Chinese provocation followed by swift and massive retaliation. The fighting spread rapidly. Beijing and its port city, Tianjin, were seized by the Japanese, and a large-scale military campaign was begun in North China.

In August, two Japanese marines were killed by Chinese troops outside Shanghai, and the Japanese landed a large expeditionary force that endangered the International Settlement. By late fall the Japanese were driving up the Yangtze River from Shanghai toward the Chinese Nationalist capital in Nanjing.

Kochu Konsu was formally dissolved in December of 1940, but it had virtually ceased functioning two years earlier. In November of 1937, much of its work was taken over by two new Japanese-inspired organizations, North China Development Corporation and Central China Development Corporation. Mantetsu transferred all its stock in Kochu Konsu to the two new companies.

Sogo did not attend the inaugural ceremony. He could point with pride to one accomplishment, a power plant that brought a reliable supply of electricity to Tianjin. At a farewell banquet in Tokyo attended by some 50 of his project managers, Sogo thanked them for their dedication and hard work.

"Our principles do not fit in with current national policies, and two other companies will take over our projects," he said. "I still believe the founding principles of Kochu Konsu will be the basis of future relations between China and Japan. Our principles have been well received by the Chinese. You will be absorbed into the new companies, but wherever you work, please uphold the ideals of Kochu Konsu. Practice them in your new assignments. Maintain your contact with loyal Chinese friends and contribute to better future relations between China and Japan."

It was to be a vain hope, as militarism continued to ride high in Japan.

有法子

CHAPTER 12

A FLING AT POLITICS

Several times during his years in government, Shinji Sogo had thought seriously of resigning and entering national politics, specifically to run for a seat in the Diet. On each occasion he had second thoughts. For one thing, his father had an intense dislike of politicians, and Shinji did not want to upset him. For another, the right opportunity never seemed to come up.

A telephone call to Sogo's home in Tokyo a few minutes after midnight on January 29, 1937, changed that. Sogo dressed and hurried to the home of his friend Kenzo Asahara, who held the reins to the Kyowa-kai political party in Manchoukuo. Asahara and two other men were waiting for him.

Over endless cups of tea, they talked until 7 a.m.

To understand the reason for this meeting, it is necessary to go back eight days to January 21 when General Juichi Terauchi, the war minister, and Diet member Kunimatsu Hamada exchanged heated words in the House of Representatives about the army's conduct. General Terauchi charged that Hamada had insulted the military. Hamada challenged the general to check the record, and if any insult were found, he said he would kill himself by ritual hara-kiri, splitting his belly with a short samurai sword. But if it were determined that there had been no insult, he demanded the general commit suicide in atonement for making false charges. Despite such melodrama, no blood flowed, but General Terauchi created such a furor that Prime Minister Koki Hirota resigned on January 23.

On January 25 General Kazushige Ugaki was given an Imperial mandate to form a new government. General Terauchi, among others, refused to let the army nominate a war minister, and without the army's support General Ugaki was unable to complete his cabinet. On January 29 General Ugaki admitted failure, and the Imperial mandate went to General Senjuro Hayashi. General Hayashi held moderate views and was not a strong man. It was widely believed he was under the influence of Colonel Kanji Ishiwara who, as a young officer, had masterminded the Shenyang Incident in 1931. In September of that year, Kwantung Army units had blown up a section of Mantetsu tracks outside Shenyang. Blaming Chinese troops, the Japanese had launched a series of attacks in "retaliation," leading ultimately to all of Manchuria coming under Japanese control.

Since then Ishiwara had taken the position that Manchoukuo must become an independent country friendly toward Japan, and the army should refrain from further aggression. Hayashi presumably would be a stopgap prime minister until

Ishiwara was ready to take over. In addition to his other short-comings Hayashi was unfamiliar with the Tokyo political scene and needed help in organizing his cabinet.

This led to the meeting at Asahara's home. Its purpose was to draw up a slate of nominees for General Hayashi's cabinet. Already there when Sogo arrived were two Manchuria special-ists, Major Tadashi Katakura and Masayoshi Miyazaki, who was a director of the Institute of Economics and Politics of Japan and Manchuria, a creation of Colonel Ishiwara. The institute's func-tion was to draw up a five-year economic plan, which had been completed but was still under study by Japan's senior statesmen.

Sogo had met General Hayashi only casually and asked why he had been included in the meeting. He was told that Hayashi was familiar with Sogo's activities, aware that he had influential friends among the Chinese and got along with moderates in the Kwantung Army, and had the kind of background necessary to win cooperation from various elements. Therefore, he was being asked—apparently by the group at the meeting—to serve as General Hayashi's chief adviser on formation of a cabinet, and to become chief cabinet secretary, a position comparable to chief of staff. The answer left Sogo only half satisfied, but he decided it would be an interesting experience to assemble a peace-making cabinet from among the nominees of various factions and agreed to take part.

After several hours Asahara received a call from General Hayashi asking him to come to his home immediately with the list of cabinet nominees proposed by Colonel Ishiwara's people. To avoid reporters waiting outside the home, Asahara disguised himself as a grocer's deliveryman and went in the back door. For the first time the prime minister designee learned that Ishiwara was recommending nominees for all the key posts, including Seishiro Itagaki as minister of war, Nobumasa Suetsugu as navy minister, and Shinji Sogo as chief adviser in forming the cabinet and chief cabinet secretary when it took office.

After Hayashi had studied the list for a while, Asahara asked whether he had any comments. Hayashi said he would like to make only one request, that Hachiro Ohashi be selected for the relatively unimportant post of director general of the Cabinet Legislation Bureau. Obviously Hayashi knew his role was puppet for the ambitious Ishiwara, but he was a good soldier and would go through with his assignment.

At 7 a.m. Sogo received a call from General Hayashi asking him to come to his home at 10 a.m. When he got there Hayashi lost no time in asking Sogo to accept the two positions that had been discussed earlier. "In order to resolve the current situation in Asia, there is no way but for Japan and China to put aside all that has happened and to work together," Hayashi said. "I believe that because you managed Mantetsu and Kochu Konsu, you are the best person to become my chief adviser for the formation of the cabinet."

Sogo demurred politely, partly because it was etiquette to decline such an offer at least three times before accepting, and partly because he was unsure how much advising he could do when Colonel Ishiwara's group seemed to be manipulating Hayashi.

"This is totally unexpected," Sogo said. "The man given the Imperial order to form a cabinet and his chief adviser must share the same principles, otherwise the process will not succeed. It is not enough to have known each other casually through business."

Hayashi took a sheet of paper from his pocket. "Asahara gave me this," Hayashi said. "I understand you helped draft it. I agree with what you have said. Let me read it to refresh your memory:

" 'The aftereffects of the Manchurian Incident must be contained within Manchuria, and we need to retain a friendly relationship with China. We are ready to cooperate with the faction within the military which shares this belief. These men were successful in stopping the Kwantung Army, which was advancing its troops across the Great Wall, just before they invaded the Tianjin area. This was a rare historical incident, and we have the same basic philosophy as these men. We believe that Manchuria should be an ideal state where the five ethnic groups live together in peace, and that the peaceful development of Manchuria depends solely on good relations with China.' "

Sogo acknowledged his support of the policy. Then, after the customary three declinations, Sogo agreed to serve Hayashi. News that Sogo had been named to head the cabinet formation advisory team astonished the press. Aside from his work with Mantetsu and the little-publicized Kochu Konsu, almost nothing was known about Sogo. Few remembered the bribery trial. Sogo was a stranger to political activity. Why had he been picked for such an important assignment?

Reporters flocked around Sogo's home asking for interviews. They found Sogo gone and no one at home except Mrs. Sogo and some of the younger children. Kiku Sogo refused to speak to the press, and eventually her third son, Kazuhei, then 18 years old, came out to meet the reporters.

"My mother," he told them, "cannot agree to a media interview without the permission of my father, and he is not here. Even if you were to interview me, I can give you no answers, because my father has not told me anything. Therefore, I am not in position even to accept your congratulations."

With that he turned and walked back into the house. "It is not clear," the magazine *Chuo Koron* said, "what the relationship is between Hayashi and Sogo . . ."

Sogo realized the need to move swiftly in organizing the Hayashi government. Within hours after his meeting with

Hayashi, Sogo set up headquarters on the second floor of the home of Shinpei Yokoyama, a former classmate of Hayashi's and one of his strong supporters.

At 5 p.m. the same day, January 30, Hayashi and Sogo met with their inner group. There they were told that Colonel Ishiwara's nominees had run into opposition. General Terauchi, the former war minister, had reported that the three members of the army's inner council, which included a prince of the royal family, wanted Lieutenant General Kotaro Nakamura as the next war minister rather than Itagaki. Although Nakamura was relatively unknown, they said Itagaki was too young; he had been promoted to lieutenant general only a few months earlier. And Isoroku Yamamoto, the vice navy minister who was to go down in history as the mastermind behind the attack on Pearl Harbor, was opposed to the appointment of Admiral Suetsugu as navy minister. He wanted another relative unknown, Vice Admiral Mitsumasa Yonai.

At 7:30 p.m. Sogo held his first press conference. He reported that disagreements within the services had delayed appointment of war and navy ministers, and all parties were reviewing their positions. The reporters made Sogo promise to meet with them whenever he left or returned to headquarters.

Sogo was on the telephone or in conference with his associates almost nonstop. At 6 a.m. on January 31 he slipped out a back door to confer with Baron Kiichiro Hiranuma, leader of a rightist political faction and a future prime minister, about some nonmilitary appointments. When Sogo returned to headquarters about 8 a.m., reporters accused him of violating their agreement.

One said: "Some of us have been watching your home. We know you didn't go there last night. Where were you, and who did you meet?"

Sogo replied: "Well, even I might have a mistress somewhere, and let's say I went there to rest a while."

Everyone burst into laughter, and Sogo hurried back to his office.

Sogo tried to impress on General Hayashi that his hopes for a cabinet that could bring peace and stability to Manchuria and China were doomed unless he could get Itagaki, with Ishiwara's backing, in as war minister. In that position, Itagaki would have the authority to curb the reckless young officers. He already has the intelligence and courage, Sogo said. After that Sogo went to see General Terauchi personally to seek some sort of compromise. Terauchi would not budge from his position that General Nakamura must be war minister.

Disconsolate, Sogo reported to Hayashi that his mission had failed. Hayashi looked up from his cup of tea and said he was inclined to accept General Terauchi's nomination, particularly since one of the officers of the inner council was a prince. Sogo pleaded with Hayashi to make one more attempt to negotiate with the generals. Reluctantly, Hayashi set out for the War Ministry, but he did not arrive when expected. Military police found his car at the residence of Prince Kan-in. After a brief visit with the prince, Hayashi went on to the War Ministry before returning to Sogo's headquarters.

"I went to see Prince Kan-in to try to get him to use his influence for our cause," Hayashi said. "Instead, he upbraided me for not accepting the decision of the council of generals. As a soldier, I have no option but to obey the wishes of an Imperial Prince."

The headquarters were in confusion. No one seemed to know what was happening. Civilian and military police milled around as did toughs known to be strong-arm agents for militant rightists. At 2 a.m. on February 1, Sogo sat down with Asahara, told him that the ideals that had brought them together had been abandoned by Hayashi, and he was prepared to resign. But,

Sogo added, since he had agreed to head the cabinet organization committee, he would complete that job before quitting. Asahara was depressed and said he, too, would resign as soon as he saw Hayashi.

But when Sogo came out of his office in the morning he found Asahara still sitting outside Hayashi's bedroom. "What happened?" Sogo asked. "Hayashi would not see me," Asahara replied. Sogo moved toward Hayashi's room when he was stopped by several guards. "Who are you?" Sogo demanded. "We are military policemen in charge of guarding the prime minister," one said. Sogo asked: "Do you know who I am?" They said they did not.

Sogo was infuriated. "I am the chairman of the Cabinet Formation Committee," he said coldly. "Guards who don't even know that don't belong here. Get out of my way."

Sogo strode into Hayashi's room and asked whether he knew Asahara had been waiting to see him all night. Hayashi replied that he knew, but wasn't seeing anyone because of a toothache. The real reason was that Asahara had been identified as a possible Communist by military secret police, and Hayashi preferred not to be seen with him.

That morning the army announced that General Nakamura had been nominated to become war minister. Once more the army had ridden roughshod over civilian government. Sogo and his friends had been defeated. Sogo was preparing to move out of committee headquarters when a secretary came to tell him that Hayashi wanted him to resign. "I was about to leave on my own accord," Sogo said. "No one needs to tell me to go."

Colonel Ishiwara called Asahara and a number of others to his office. He wanted to protect them from possible arrest by military police until the tension eased.

Soon after the Hayashi cabinet took office, Itagaki was transferred to a post in Hiroshima where he was out of the mainstream of political activity. But not for long. He would be back for a key role in the next political turnover. Colonel Ishiwara was promoted to major general, perhaps in recognition of his abilities, and assigned briefly to the general staff office with some responsibility for cooperating with Sogo's Kochu Konsu. After that he was assigned to the Kwantung Army in Manchuria, then under command of ambitious General Hideki Tojo with whom he was destined to clash. The new minister of war, Nakamura, was soon incapacitated by typhoid fever. And the Hayashi government lasted only four months before it was succeeded by Prince Fumimaro Konoye and his "national union" cabinet with Koki Hirota back as foreign minister. Lieutenant General Sugiyama, another old-timer and associate of Terauchi, became war minister with the hawkish Yoshijiro Umezu as vice minister.

An analyst wrote: "The Hayashi cabinet was a floating cabinet which had been cut off from both the War Ministry and the political parties. During the process of forming the cabinet, it became clear there were serious disagreements within the military, between the Manchuria faction headed by Colonel Ishiwara and a new faction headed by a young lieutenant general named Hideki Tojo."

For the first time Tojo was identified prominently among the plotters and players in Japan's political power struggle. He was commander of the Kwantung Army, but he had broader horizons. He saw Japan's Axis ties with Germany and Italy as a valuable asset in long-range strategy.

When Ishiwara was assigned to the Kwantung Army under Tojo, an observer noted that the two generals were in the same boat but had conflicting ideas about which way it should go. Ishiwara's goal was to consolidate Japan's position in Manchuria and build a prosperous nation. Tojo had ambitious ideas about expanding Japan's hold on the mainland at China's expense. It was inevitable they should clash.

In May of 1938 Prime Minister Konoye shook up his cabinet. It was called "cabinet reform," but army and navy officers took over six portfolios, with General Kazushige Ugaki becoming foreign minister. Significantly, Konoye ignored the objection of the army and named General Seishiro Itagaki, over whose failed appointment Sogo had quit the Hayashi camp, as his new war minister.

When Vice Minister Umezu heard of the shake-up he hurriedly resigned and went outside of channels to name General Tojo as his own successor. Itagaki took office as war minister on June 3 and found Tojo already sitting at the vice minister's desk.

Back in Manchoukuo, General Ishiwara was Tojo's logical successor as commander of the Kwantung Army, but Tojo managed to appoint Lieutenant General Rensuke Isogai, his close associate and advocate of expansion into North China, to the position. Ishiwara soon found it impossible to reconcile their differences. After two months, Ishiwara, who was having kidney problems, asked that his resignation from the army be accepted and that he be transferred to the reserves.

When Ishiwara returned to Japan for medical treatment, he was depicted by some of his enemies as a deserter and Communist sympathizer. The army's secret police went so far as to gather "evidence" of subversion against Ishiwara, but War Minister Itagaki refused to consider charges. Sogo was among those who went to see Ishiwara. He took the position that there was a plot to oust Ishiwara, that his decision to resign was due to illness and not of his free will, and that he should be hospitalized before any further action was taken.

One night Vice Minister Tojo confronted Itagaki with a demand that the Ishiwara issue be brought to a conclusion. Fed up, Itagaki took courageous action. He demoted Tojo after only six months as vice minister, and assigned Ishiwara as commander of the army garrison at Maizuru on the west coast of Japan, opposite the Korean Peninsula.

The confusing shuffling of personalities was part of the deadly power struggle in a nominally civilian government that was dominated by a cast of ruthless and ambitious militarists. The civilian leadership, such as it was, was virtually helpless as the nation sank ever deeper into the morass of its own China policy. As for Sogo, his experience with Hayashi disillusioned him about politics and left him deeply troubled about the course his country was taking. He returned to Manchuria to do what he could with Kochu Konsu. When it was absorbed into the North China Development Company, Sogo returned to Japan, perhaps permanently, to rest and think.

有法子

CHAPTER 13

PEARL HARBOR

Shinji Sogo's return to Japan in 1939 was less than triumphant. He was jobless at 55, feeling frustrated and useless. Although 55 was the normal retirement age for ordinary Japanese at the time, men in important positions could continue working almost indefinitely, and certainly Sogo was a man of stature. He has spent some of his most vigorous years on the Asian mainland as a high-ranking executive of the South Manchuria Railway. But Kochu Konsu, his idealistic dream for Japanese-Chinese-Manchurian economic cooperation, had been thwarted at every turn by aggressive elements in the Kwantung Army and their civilian supporters. Sogo's goal of bringing Northeast Asia's five ethnic groups together in peace—Japanese, Manchus, Mongolians, Korean, and Chinese—had gotten nowhere. His single venture into political leadership had failed almost before it began. Having been so completely discredited, was his productive life over?

In his heart Sogo knew he was too restless, too concerned about the future of his country, which under a virtual military dictatorship had become hopelessly and helplessly mired in the vastness and near-chaos of the Asian continent, to fade quietly into retirement.

Since there seemed to be no opportunity to enter government, what could he do from the outside to influence national policy? It would be extremely difficult to have his voice heard in such a time, and besides he had no specific ideas. For the time being he decided to enjoy his family and the natural and historical attractions of his own country, which he had had little time to get to know. With friends and family he spent many weeks visiting historic sites and scenic areas, making leisurely stops in peaceful country inns, and enjoying the relaxation of hot spring spas.

One day his travels took him to mountainous Ibaraki Prefecture where the Student Volunteer Army, a national service youth corps to support the war effort, had a training center. His old friend Kanji Kato headed the organization. University students were still exempted from military service, but many of them were joining the Volunteer Army to work during vacations and weekends on construction projects.

Sogo liked what he saw of these youths. They, he realized, rather than the military, should be Japan's leaders when the war on the mainland was over. When he was invited to address a group of the volunteers, Sogo expressed some views that were unusual for the times.

"Tomorrow's leaders," Sogo told the youths, "must maintain

the principles of freedom for all people, if Japan is to find peace and prosperity. Power must come from the citizens themselves and not be seized by a few."

This kind of message was alien to everything students were taught in their schools where they were being indoctrinated in the idea that it was proper and necessary for every aspect of their lives to be controlled and regulated by those in authority. But if Sogo's views alarmed sponsors of the volunteer movement, that did not prevent his appointment in the fall of 1941 as chairman of a reorganized group called the Student Volunteer Association. The change from "Volunteer Army" to "Volunteer Association" was more important than appeared on the surface. Sogo set out to replace military-type discipline with a more liberal outlook. One of his first actions was to open his Tokyo home to members for weekly discussion sessions.

Although membership was nationwide, the concentration of colleges and universities in Tokyo meant there were many of these student volunteers in the capital. "As many as 60 students would attend these sessions," Sogo once recalled. "They were very serious. They were patriotic young Japanese but worried about the future of their country, and I lost no opportunity to stimulate their thinking. They held heated discussions, and through them many national service work projects were born. When they decided to undertake a project, the students took the initiative for recruiting help from other schools. We held to the principle that all people who wanted to serve the nation in an informal capacity would work as volunteers."

It was inevitable that so many students gathering at Sogo's home regularly should arouse the suspicion of police, who were on diligent lookout for Communists and other dissidents. When they interrupted a meeting, the police were surprised to be invited to participate in the planning and take part in discussions about the future of the country.

Because of the nationwide labor shortage, volunteer help was welcomed everywhere, particularly on construction projects, many of which had come to a standstill. In rugged Shiga Prefecture west of Tokyo student volunteers worked on building Serikawa Dam. In communities where most of the young men had been drafted into military service, they undertook heavy work like planting trees, clearing land, and digging drainage ditches. The volunteers slept on straw mats in schoolhouses and took turns preparing simple meals for the work crews. Sogo was pleased to see that in time elderly villagers, moved by the volunteer spirit, came forward to help with kitchen chores so more of the youths were freed for heavy work.

In other totalitarian countries, such as Nazi Germany, Italy, and the Soviet Union, youth corps were set up to promote the regime's political ideology as well as provide voluntary labor. Sogo, who had seen his fill of militarism in Manchuria and China, promoted patriotism while encouraging independent thought about Japan's future role in Asia. Often he visited field-work sites and took his turn at hard labor. One of his visits took Sogo to Izu where student volunteers were mining coal alongside conscripted Korean laborers and Chinese prisoners of war, who, under provisions of the Geneva Convention, could not be forced into strategic work. It is not likely that Sogo was aware of this regulation, and besides, if Japanese student volunteers could handle the labor, why should it be considered illegal to put Chinese prisoners to work? Years later, after the Japanese surrender, this episode led to Sogo being accused as a war criminal by American Occupation forces. (See Chapter 15.)

Pearl Harbor Day, December 8, 1941, in Japan, still recalled so vividly in the United States where the nation was jolted abruptly into war, is regarded with relatively less significance among the Japanese. For them it was just the opening of another chapter in a long series of unpleasantness in a war that seemed to have no end. The nation already was suffering shortages of food, clothing, and other necessities. Luxuries had disappeared long ago. Young men were being sent off to fight in distant parts of the Asian mainland. Increasing numbers of little wooden boxes wrapped in white cloth, containing the ashes of soldiers killed in China, were returning to the homeland. The people were weary of being exhorted to sacrifice endlessly for the national glory.

In the summer of 1941 they were told that the U.S. had imposed an embargo on sales of oil and steel to Japan unless it withdrew from China. That would mean all the sacrifice of the previous decade would have been in vain. And it was obvious that a country that depended heavily on imports of such strategic materials soon would be strangled. If Japan's dreams of empire were to survive, open confrontation with the U.S. seemed inevitable. The primary question was when and how.

Among many of the elderly, the events of that December day are hardly remembered. Some have recollections that the state-owned radio network played stirring martial music before announcing that the Imperial navy's planes had attacked Hawaii with devastating effect. But few recall their thoughts—either elation over a military victory or fear that the war was being expanded—on the day that marked the beginning of Japan's downfall.

Sogo himself rarely spoke of that event. He left no record of his thoughts, and there is no way to tell how he felt. But some of his surviving contemporaries, when pressed, say they "*hotto shita*," an expression indicating they felt relief—relief that their national leaders had taken a significant action to break the seemingly interminable and costly military stalemate in China. Regardless of how military aggression on the mainland had mired the nation in one problem after another, there was no widespread sense of guilt in pursuing the war in whatever way was necessary. To the contrary, the Japanese people had been made well aware of the way that the so-called ABCD Alliance—America, Britain, China, and the Dutch in the East Indies—was tightening an economic noose around a Japan facing increasing shortages of food and fuel. The Japanese saw the ABCD Alliance as just another part of the plot by ex-imperialist Western nations to block her rightful aspirations.

The attack on Pearl Harbor, opening up a new dimension to the war already raging in Europe and the Asian mainland, was seen by many in Japan as its only alternative to fatal strangulation. It is not unreasonable to think that Sogo felt his work with the Student Volunteer Association was his significant contribution to the war effort.

One day in the spring of 1943 Sogo was asked whether his volunteers could be sent to lay railroad track on the far northern island of Sakhalin, called *Karafuto* in Japanese. The southern half of this long, narrow island had been ceded to Japan as part of the settlement of the Russo-Japanese War in 1905, with Russia retaining the northen half. The Soviet Union had always been considered an unreliable neighbor, and Tokyo felt the need for improving transportation facilities in case trouble broke out despite their nonaggression pact. Much of *Karafuto* was tundra, the climate was harsh, and there were few settlements. Sogo was hesitant about asking his students to take on the assignment, but more than 2,000 youths from all parts of Japan volunteered. Seven hundred were selected. They paid their expenses to Tokyo where they were placed aboard a special train and taken by rail and ferry to the island of Hokkaido, where they boarded a ship for *Karafuto*.

Sogo visited their camp late that summer and found his volunteers were doing an outstanding job of clearing land, pulling stumps, preparing a roadbed, and laying track. What pleased him even more was that at the end of a long day of labor the students still had enough energy to hold discussion sessions on how best they could serve their nation. The railroad project was completed by the time heavy frost set in. By then, regardless of what the idealistic volunteers might have had in mind for their next national service project, their government had made the decision for them. On December 1, 1943, draft exemption for college students was discontinued. Most of the volunteers throughout the nation were conscripted, and, in view of the staggering casualty rate suffered by Japanese troops in the late stages of the war, it can be assumed that huge numbers of them died.

Shinji Sogo's own family did not escape sorrow. His first child, Kosaku, born in 1908, was among the casualties. Kosaku had been graduated from the elite Kyoto Imperial University in 1932 and joined the giant Mitsubishi Corporation. In 1935 he married Miyoko Obata, daughter of Major General Toshishiro Obata, who then headed the national military academy and later became minister of home affairs. General Sadao Araki served in the traditional role of go-between in arranging the marriage. A daughter and a son were born to Kosaku and Miyoko.

In May of 1942 Kosaku was en route to Java on a ship chartered by Mitsubishi when it was attacked and sunk by a submarine somewhere in the South China Sea. Because of censorship Shinji did not learn of the attack until some time later.

When he finally got the news Shinji hurried to Mitsubishi's offices to learn what he could. He was told that most of those aboard the sunken ship had survived, but one lifeboat—the boat Kosaku was on—was missing. It was many more days before the lifeboat, with all aboard dead, was found grounded on a remote island. The remains were flown back to the port of Hakata in Kyushu, the southernmost island in the Japanese homeland. Shinji identified his son by the cigarette case in a pocket of his jacket. Kosaku had enjoyed smoking, and because of the tobacco shortage he would smoke only part of a cigarette and save the stubs for another time. There were many stubs in the case, and Shinji took that to mean his son had not lived long after the attack.

At the funeral service in Sogo's home, priests from four Nichiren Buddhist sects came to chant sutras in Kosaku's memory. For years after their son's death, Shinji and his wife, Kiku, continued the practice of chanting sutras each night to console Kosaku's soul in the afterlife. Their third son, Kazuhei, who was still a university student in Sendai, remembers hearing his parents chanting late into the night whenever he came home.

"I don't recall how long they continued the nightly services," he once said, "but I could understand their sorrow. At other times I became angry at them for not accepting Kosaku's death more stoically, but now that I am older, I can understand how deeply they were hurt by the loss of their son."

有法子

CHAPTER 14

THE PLOT

By the middle of 1944, the war news was far from encouraging for Japan. The momentum had changed drastically. After Pearl Harbor, the first attacks in 1942 had carried Japanese forces across Southeast Asia almost to the borders of India, raising hopes that before long the United States and Great Britain would seek some sort of settlement with Japan so they could concentrate on the war in Europe. On the south, Australia was desperately preparing for a possible Japanese invasion. Most of the islands in the southwest Pacific were in Japanese hands, and a token landing had been made in the Aleutians in the North Pacific.

But by the time the tide turned, Japanese supply lines were stretched to the breaking point. U.S. submarines were taking a heavy toll on Japanese freighters and troop transports. With American industrial production in high gear, well-armed Allied forces were slowly taking back lost territory in one bloody campaign after another, demonstrating courage and fighting skill the Japanese had not anticipated.

In the Battle of Midway in June of 1942, Japan lost four critically needed aircraft carriers. The Japanese navy, which was the key to the nation's military power, never recovered from that setback. Several months later, U.S. forces retook the island of Guadalcanal, seizing Japan's major air base in the southwest Pacific and crippling Japanese operations in that vast area. On the mainland, long convoys of U.S. trucks began moving supplies from India over the Burma Road to bolster Chinese troops. Little of this news filtered through the censorship, but people like Sogo could sense the noose tightening as, island by island and mile by mile, Japanese troops pulled back toward the homeland.

Sogo, with no duties other than to supervise the Volunteer Association, was restless. Thus, he was pleased when one day Kenzo Asahara, who in 1937 had persuaded Sogo to take part in the ill-fated effort to help General Senjuro Hayashi establish a government, introduced him to a charismatic young military officer. His name was Tomoshige Tsunoda, a major attached to Imperial headquarters in Tokyo. It was a meeting that before long led to Sogo's involvement in a bizarre plot which, had it been attempted and failed, could have cost him his life.

Although he seldom talked about this experience, in later years Sogo had many occasions to wonder how he had allowed himself to become part of such a dangerous scheme so foreign to his way of life. And he could find no answer other than his love for his country.

Tsunoda had graduated at the top of his military academy class in 1941. His first post was in the dangerous, mountainous area of North China. In addition to Tsunoda's military skills, there may have been other factors involved in his rapid promotion to the rank of major and his transfer before long to Tokyo headquarters. His blood lines were exceptional. He was the third son of former Major General Koreshige Tsunoda, who had served in the Russo-Japanese War, had been a superintendent of the military academy where one of his students had been Hideki Tojo, and had been elected to the lower house of the Diet after leaving the army.

After a year in the frontier post, Tsunoda was assigned to headquarters in Nanjing. There he found growing uneasiness about Prime Minister (and General) Tojo's ability to cope with the growing American power in the war then raging. It is likely, although unconfirmable, that Tsunoda met Prince Mikasa, youngest brother of Emperor Hirohito, who was a staff officer attached to Nanjing headquarters during that period. This becomes significant because recently uncovered documents reveal that the prince (protected by his Imperial status) created quite a stir when in a lecture to staff officers he criticized the army's aggression in China. Such an opinion, openly voiced by a member of the Imperial Family, could not but have had an enormous impact on the officer corps.

In May of 1944, with American forces advancing ever closer to the Japanese homeland, Tsunoda was brought back to Imperial headquarters in Tokyo. There was not a great deal for him to do, and Tsunoda had access to a vast file of documents and plenty of time to pore over them.

Presently, he discovered that a surprising number of intelligence reports and analyses produced before the attack on Pearl Harbor had warned that Japan would suffer heavy damage in any war with the U.S. and ultimately would face defeat. Now it was only too evident that these predictions were well founded. Tsunoda, like many others in the still-silent leadership, could see that it was well enough to speak of the indomitable Japanese spirit overcoming American guns and ships and planes and bombs, but realistically defeat was inevitable. What could be done to minimize the impact?

In July of 1944 Major Tsunoda secretly wrote a paper innocuously titled "An Observation About the Current Situation in the Great East Asia War." In essence, it was a proposal for getting rid of Tojo, preferably by persuasion but by violence, if it came to that, and replacing him as prime minister with a member of the Imperial Family, who presumably could unite Japan's various military and civilian factions.

If the plot sounds far-fetched, even as the brainchild of an overzealous junior army officer, it must be remembered that Japan has a history of fanatical young men risking their lives to seek drastic political goals. Less than ten years earlier, in the uprising on February 26, 1936, it was a clique of young army officers who, in the Emperor's name, spearheaded a futile revolt against civilian leadership. A number of cabinet ministers were slain before the attempted coup was put down.

There is no indication that anyone other than Major Tsunoda was involved in formulating his plot. He carefully outlined his strategy and made nine copies of the document. One he kept. The others were to be shared with coconspirators as they were brought into the plan. Major Tsunoda's strategy was to involve eight others: Prince Mikasa; Prince Takamatsu; Sogo's friend Kenzo Asahara, who was a leader of the Kyowa-Kai political party in Manchoukuo; Sogo's friend Kanji Kato, who had brought him into the Student Volunteer movement; former Major General Kanji Ishiwara, who had helped Sogo to organize the Kochu Konsu economic development plan for China and had resigned from the army in protest against its aggressions;

Tatsukuma Ushijima, a Tokyo businessman who was a judo expert and Asahara's best friend; Sogo; and Toshishiro Obata, head of the national military academy and father-in-law of Sogo's eldest son. Thus, it would seem Sogo was recruited mainly because he happened to be well acquainted with four of the men chosen to become members of Major Tsunoda's inner circle.

The first to be brought into Major Tsunoda's plan was Ushijima, whose role was the key to the plot. Ushijima somehow was to gain access to Tojo and demand his resignation. If Tojo refused, Ushijima was to kill him.

Apparently Ushijima needed little persuading. After he agreed to the plot, he and Major Tsunoda visited General Ishiwara, who was keeping a low profile in rural Yamagata Prefecture in the northern part of the country. As they explained their plot, it was plain to Ishiwara that he would lose his life if the insurrection failed. But he did not hesitate to say he would back it. He had a warning for the conspirators: "Members of the Imperial Family have not been brought up to fight for causes at the risk of their lives. Be careful. You may be disappointed if your plan hinges entirely on them."

Major Tsunoda thanked him for the advice and assured the old general he would be cautious. Then, elated by the general's support, Major Tsunoda and Ushijima returned to Tokyo and called Obata and Sogo together to a teahouse to reveal their plans. Obata was the more outspoken but also the more cautious of the two. When his visitors' voices rose in their enthusiasm, Obata warned: "Watch out. You never know where Tojo's agents are." Then he said he supported the plan but declined to commit himself to any particular role.

Sogo did not know quite what to do. He surmised that he was being included not only because he opposed the military but because he had many friends in the civilian bureaucracy whose support was necessary if the country were to function after the coup. Violence and intrigue were alien to his nature. He still remembered the frustration of the campaign to install General Hayashi as prime minister. Yet he was deeply disturbed with what the Kwantung Army had done in Manchuria and North China and aware that Tojo had done nothing to show he could stave off total disaster. Sogo agreed to support the plot without knowing exactly what he would, or could, do.

Step by step, Major Tsunoda expanded his network. He met secretly with Prince Mikasa and apparently won his tacit support. Kanji Kato, after he was brought into the plot, was assigned to talk to Prince Takamatsu. Sogo's friend Kenzo Asahara was in Shanghai where he was reached by mail. In a coded telegraphic response, he pledged his support.

Because no copies of Major Tsunoda's document have survived, there is no record of the way he proposed to carry out his plan other than that Ushijima was to be the trigger man, who would confront Tojo and demand his resignation. It is not clear whether Ushijima's approach was to be an appeal to reason or a threat of violence, or what the plotters would do if Tojo and his men reacted violently. Would Ushijima have sacrificed his life to Tojo's bodyguard by killing him on the spot? Had some members of Tojo's personal guard been compromised by Major Tsunoda? Would the army respond to General Ishiwara's leadership? And what were Sogo and other members of the plot to do when Tojo was out of the way?

None of this is known, and in any event Tsunoda's plot, which was scheduled to be put into motion on July 25, 1944, abruptly became irrelevant. Tojo and his cabinet, overwhelmed by one military setback after another, resigned on their own exactly one week before the day set for the uprising. General Kuniaki Koiso became prime minister and Admiral Mitsumasa Yonai deputy prime minister. By then the Axis Alliance was in a shambles. A year earlier, Benito Mussolini had resigned with his cabinet in Italy and was placed under arrest. The Allied invasion of Normandy had been launched June 6, and U.S. columns were driving into France. The Germans were being savaged by Allied bombers day and night and battered in a two-front land war with Russians pounding the eastern front. The question now was how long Japan could hold out.

In a strange turn of events, the first part of Major Tsunoda's objective, to oust Tojo, had been reached peacefully and properly without bloodshed. As General Koiso sought to bring order to his government, most of Tsunoda's conspirators discretely destroyed their documents.

Accounts differ as to what happened after that, but apparently word of Tsunoda's plot was leaked to the military police, possibly by Prince Mikasa, who feared for the future of his country. The head of the military police—with broad internal security powers—was Colonel Ryoji Shikata, one of Tojo's henchmen. On September 3 they arrested Tsunoda, then picked up Ushijima and Asahara shortly afterward.

The homes of Obata and Sogo were searched, but apparently nothing incriminating was found. Kazuhei Sogo remembers the family received a call from the military police saying they were coming to search the house. A group of soldiers, who presumably had been watching the Sogo home from the second floor of a neighbor's house, arrived within minutes. At General Ishiwara's home the police found a copy of Major Tsunoda's plans—believed to be the only copy remaining—but it, too, has vanished over the years.

For some reason, the charges Colonel Shikata filed depicted Asahara, rather than Major Tsunoda, as the leader of the plot. Asahara was found guilty in a court-martial and hustled off to a military prison to await sentencing. Strangely, none of the others served prison sentences.

General Ishiwara was summoned to a court-martial but was released, perhaps in deference to his military service. Tsunoda was stripped of his military commission and given a two-year prison term which, strangely, was suspended. After all, he may have been plotting against Tojo, but the evidence was skimpy, and the plot was never carried out. Under other circumstances he could very well have been executed.

Obata was summoned for trial but was released. Sogo was never charged, but for a long time afterward friends warned him to be careful about where he went and what he did. "The Tojo faction will try to kill you," he was warned. "You must not give them a chance to do it." If Sogo was worried, he showed no signs of it.

Why was Asahara alone imprisoned? One conjecture is that he was particularly close to General Ishiwara, whose opposition to Tojo was well known. And since it was awkward to punish the general in view of his record of military service to his country, Tojo's clique took out their frustration on Asahara. Asahara was released from prison in January 1945. Sogo took him and his wife to his home in Tokyo, where they rested for some weeks before moving to the dubious safety of Shanghai. Some time later Tsunoda, who also feared assassination, joined Asahara in Shanghai. After the war Tsunoda became a television network executive and an adviser to *Shinano Mainichi*, a daily newspaper. He died in 1987 at age 70.

This strange episode in Japanese history is little known. Because the revolt was never carried out, few today are aware the plot existed. The history of Japan is replete with political plots, many of which never went beyond the planning stage, and Tsunoda's plan for unseating the Tojo regime may be considered one of them. Yet, it seems remarkable that the military police, whose agents were everywhere and who had a reputation for brutality and ruthlessness, did not press for harsher punishment of Tsunoda and his conspirators. No publicity was given the court-martial, and those involved were reluctant to talk, at the time or later. If this episode came to the attention of U.S. Occupation officials, apparently it was never out in the open when Sogo was questioned about alleged war crimes.

As it turned out, what Major Tsunoda sought to accomplish by violence if necessary came to pass in the course of events. Admiral Koiso, who replaced Tojo as prime minister, resigned after only eight months following the huge American invasion of Okinawa that was launched on April 1. Now, for the first time, the enemy was fighting on Japanese soil.

Koiso was replaced by Admiral Kantaro Suzuki, who for many years after retirement from the navy had been Grand Chamberlain, that is, Adviser to the Emperor. Admiral Suzuki was prime minister at the time of Japan's surrender. His job was done after the surrender ceremonies on the American battleship *Missouri*, and he was ready to step down. A few days later he was succeeded by Prince Higashikuni. Japan's civilian peace faction had considered Higashikuni for the prime minister's post before the outbreak of war, because, as one observer put it, "nothing short of the authority of a prince of the Imperial blood at the head of the cabinet could curb the excesses of the militarists." But because of the possibility that war against the U.S. would break out regardless, Tojo was named prime minister to avoid involving the Imperial Family. After the surrender, Prince Higashikuni was asked to form a cabinet. In the delicate terms employed by Shigeru Yoshida, foreign minister in Higashikuni's cabinet and later a prime minister, the prince was to "exert the authority of his position to override any objections which the army might have to carrying out the measures made necessary by the circumstances in which the war came to a close."

Thus, in a belated and roundabout way, Major Tsunoda's goal of installing a member of the Imperial Family as head of government was realized. But even as Tsunoda pursued his plot, it was apparent the war was lost. Italy had surrendered, and German armies were in full retreat. The main Japanese cities were in ashes from repeated air raids, and it was obvious the Yanks were preparing for an early invasion of the Japanese homeland itself.

Admiral Suzuki's job was to try and hold the country together while others negotiated a peace.

It is a tribute to Japanese stubbornness, or evidence of Japanese inability to face reality, that even under such devastating circumstances the military leadership was preparing for a fight to the finish on the home islands. Part of the strategy was to establish an emergency rail transportation headquarters away from Tokyo to be used in case of invasion. The site chosen was on the relatively undeveloped and unbombed island of Shikoku where Sogo had been born and spent his boyhood. About the same time a new line was being opened on Shikoku. And because things must be done properly, even under dire circumstances, there had to be a proper ceremony for dedicating the line.

Since important Transportation Ministry officials could not be spared, it was suggested Sogo be asked to represent the government at the dedication. For Sogo, who wanted to get out of Tokyo and was anxious to see his birthplace again, it sounded like a fine idea, and he agreed to go.

有法子

CHAPTER 15

AFTER THE SURRENDER

Saijo, a town of 30,000 on Shikoku Island and separated from the Japanese mainland by the Seto Inland Sea, had escaped the damage inflicted by air raids on larger communities and most of the trauma of a war that was not going well. Aside from the young men getting red-paper draft notices and going off to serve in uniform, war had brought relatively little change in the easy tempo of rural life. The opening of the new railway line was carried out with due ceremony in late June of 1945. Afterward, local dignitaries and Sogo, the honored guest from Tokyo, adjourned, as was traditional, to a restaurant for a banquet.

During the conversation Sogo learned Saijo had attained

legal status as a city early in 1941 with the mayor being chosen by the city council. But now times were changing, and it
might be appropriate to seek another mayor. Would Sogo be
interested?

There was no question about Sogo's popularity or his
qualifications. The issue, as one elder put it, was: "Can a big
pine tree from the banks of the Kamo River become a bonsai
in Saijo?"

Sogo was intrigued with the idea of moving to Saijo. He liked
the prospect of going back to work—although he was not anxious
to return to Tokyo. Taking a lesser post than he had been accustomed to did not bother him at all. He was living on a pension
that was more than enough to meet his modest needs in a place
like Saijo, and it seemed unlikely the military police would
bother him if he stayed out of the limelight in a country town.
Without consulting his wife Kiku—he seldom bothered her
with the need to make family decisions—he told his Saijo
friends he would be happy to become mayor, if three conditions
could be agreed upon:

First, he said, he would not accept a salary or any benefits
usually attached to the mayor's office.

Second, he would be free to resign any time the national
government invited his services.

Third, he could resign if even a single citizen opposed his
decisions as mayor. The implication was that if they wanted to
retain his services, the citizens should keep their complaints to
themselves.

Those were terms the city council could not turn down.
Although Kiku had no voice in the matter, she welcomed the
opportunity to leave Tokyo. Sogo returned to Saijo in mid-July.
It was well that he did, for within two months Tokyo was to be
in near-chaos as Occupation troops landed, taking over some of
the remaining office buildings for headquarters and many of the

better homes for the use of high-ranking officers. In Saijo he rented a house near the railroad station. A city official called on Sogo and offered to pay the rent. Sogo sent him packing. Before long Kiku and Sogo's niece, Takiko Kudo, who would help with running the household, joined him.

Life in Saijo was pleasant. He was welcomed as a local boy who had made good and come home. Citizens brought the Sogos gifts of fresh fish and fruits and vegetables. Sogo's favorite tangerines, scarce in Tokyo, were plentiful in Saijo. Despite wartime rationing, there even seemed to be an adequate supply of sugar, and Takiko Kudo fixed him the sweets that he loved. Sometimes, like a child, he even sprinkled sugar over his rice.

Sogo was wise enough not to become involved in daily matters at the city offices. He simply called in various department heads, told them he had confidence in their abilities, and ordered them to use their best judgment and do what needed to be done. "I will accept full responsibility for what you decide to do," he said, knowing that such trust would encourage them to do their best.

On August 15, 1945, two weeks after he took office, Sogo was notified from Tokyo that all city employees must assemble for a special announcement to be broadcast on the national radio network. Sogo had a fair idea about what was to happen, but he was unaware of the details. At the appointed hour, the city employees lined up in ranks behind Mayor Sogo in the plaza outside city hall waiting for a radio on a table to come to life.

"At first," a city employee recalled, "we could not understand the message that started coming over the radio. It was a strange voice, and the form of language was unfamiliar, not the everyday kind of language ordinary Japanese would use. The mayor stood stiffly at attention in front of us, and then his shoulders began to sag. We realized he was starting to cry. Then we knew that our country had surrendered to the Allies, and the war was over. Presently the mayor dabbed at his eyes, regained his composure, told us to be courageous and good citizens, and sent us home. Only later did we realize the voice we had heard on the radio was the voice of the Emperor telling us we Japanese had lost the war and now must be prepared to bear the unbearable."

American aircraft stopped flying high over Saijo on their way to bombing targets. Word was received that U.S. troops were coming ashore unopposed in other parts of Japan. In Saijo there was concern and dread, but nothing unusual took place. The consequences of the surrender, as of the war itself, were far away. Sogo, leaving the routine of city government to the regular employees, soon applied himself to what he perceived as Saijo's two most pressing long-term needs.

The first was a better education program so the city's young people would be prepared to cope with the changes Sogo knew were coming. The national education system was highly centralized, with direction coming from Tokyo. Sogo understood he could do nothing about that, but there were ways of stimulating local initiative and developing local programs to help children be qualified to take their places in society. He organized monthly meetings for the teachers and administrators from Saijo's 13 schools to discuss ways of enhancing the directives from the Ministry of National Education.

The second was to ensure Saijo's economy, primarily by increasing its agricultural output and providing better ways to get the produce to market. The strategy he devised was complex and, as it turned out, staggeringly expensive.

The city of Saijo is located on a narrow plain between the Shikoku mountain range and the Seto Inland Sea. Arable land is scarce. Further, 11 different streams carrying the abundant rainfall from the mountains to the sea frequently flooded the Saijo area. Sogo asked civil engineers from the Ministry of

Transportation to recommend ways of preventing floods and protecting rice fields.

They found the stream channels choked with sand and gravel and recommended an extensive dredging program to clear the way to the sea. It would be simple enough to dredge the riverbeds, but where would the sand and gravel be dumped without covering up valuable farmland? Sogo asked around and learned that a prefectural project to build a badly needed section of highway between Saijo and the city of Matsuyama had been suspended because of cost. Sogo visited the governor, offered to provide the fill for the new highway without charge, and persuaded him to complete the project. Then he mobilized volunteers in Saijo to help move sand and rocks from streambed to roadway. The result: better highway transportation for Saijo, streambed improvement, and less possibility of flooding.

This was cause for rejoicing, but Sogo had more ambitious plans. In his youth, the town of Saijo was handicapped by the lack of a harbor. It had a beautiful sandy beach, but the water was so shallow that even at high tide ships could not approach the shore. Freight and passengers bound for Honshu were ferried in horse-drawn wagons through the water to boats waiting far offshore. Now, as mayor, Sogo realized Saijo would never become an important or prosperous city without shipping links to Honshu markets. Thus it was that he came up with an ambitious plan to create a tidal basin for docking ships while at the same time increasing land available for farming.

Basic to the plan was construction of a breakwater about a mile and a quarter long, extending at a sharp angle from the shore out into the sea. The beach on the seaward end of the breakwater would be excavated for a sheltered anchorage basin. The excavated sand and rocks would be packed behind the breakwater on the landward side and topped with soil. In this way Saijo would acquire both an anchorage and additional farmland. The trouble was that since the project would require a huge investment to build dikes and floodgates and move hundreds of thousands of tons of sand, rock, and soil, it was too large a project for Saijo City alone.

Sogo brought together officials from the city, the Ehime Prefectural government, and the Ministry of Agriculture and won promises of support for a project that would benefit all of them. Then he went to the construction department of Sumitomo Kogyo Company Ltd., which later became the giant Sumitomo Construction Company, to talk about detailed planning and getting the job under way. The cost of labor at the time was ¥20 per day, and labor alone for the project was estimated to run as high as ¥7.5 million. The total budget had been set at only ¥4.3 million.

Sogo had to use his best persuasive skills to win the support of all involved. One of his proposals, which Sumitomo turned down, was a schedule of deferred payments which would be met by selling the rice to be grown years later on the reclaimed lands. In the end, Sumitomo agreed to take over as the general contractor, Ehime Prefecture provided a subsidy, farmers pledged to donate rice, and Saijo City became the coordinator.

After surveys were started, it was found that costs would be slashed by using a new engineering technique employing dredging pumps. The pumps saved labor and reduced construction time, but much of the savings were eaten up by an unexpected factor—inflation. Workmen's wages, which were ¥20 a day when the project was begun, soared tenfold in a short time.

During this period Sogo was visiting Tokyo frequently to confer with government officials. On one of these trips Sogo was asked to take over as chairman of the Tetsudo Kosai-kai, a foundation responsible for the welfare of retired National Railways employees and the families of workers killed or disabled in line of duty. War's end had left Tetsudo Kosai-kai in difficult straits. Most of its income came from shops and newsstands in railroad stations. With the economy depressed, travelers spent little at the stands. Disruption in rail service also contributed to slashing the income of these stores. Dilapidated rolling stock and safety equipment was responsible for an unexpected number of accidents, which led to deaths and injuries straining Kosai-kai's resources. Kosai-kai was having difficulty paying the salaries of its 1,000 employees.

Sogo could not ignore the pleas of friends in the Railways Ministry. In April of 1946, less than a year after becoming mayor of Saijo, Sogo told the city council he was resigning to assume responsibilities affecting the entire nation. Start of construction on the breakwater project was still some months in the future, but Sogo was confident all was in order. Construction began on January 10, 1947, more than eight months after Sogo's departure. The first crop of rice from the reclaimed area was harvested in the fall of 1950 when Japan was still experiencing rice shortages. A sack of the initial harvest was presented with great ceremony to Takeyuki Saito, the Sumitomo executive who had committed his company to the project. It was a deep-felt token of appreciation to Saito for his consistent support in spite of the inflation that had cost his company millions.

At Kosai-kai Sogo found the problems more difficult than he had anticipated. Trackage, rolling stock, bridges, and safety equipment had deteriorated badly during the war years, and there was very little material to repair or replace them. Even on main lines, replacing unsafe old rails usually was a matter of finding and installing rails only slightly less worn. Accidents were frequent. In 1946 an astonishing 46,578 accidents were reported, and many more simply went unrecorded.

In February of 1947 an accident attributable to faulty equipment resulted in nearly 700 casualties. A train, loaded with city dwellers bound for farm areas in hopes of bartering family treasures for food for their families, was derailed near the Korai

River. Investigation revealed the locomotive's speedometer had not been functioning. Early in the run the brakes had been causing problems. The wooden cars had been packed with passengers. On a downgrade the brakes failed to respond, and the train flew off the tracks on a curve.

There were demands for improved rail service, but Allied Occupation policies made a quick fix difficult. The best cars, about one-tenth of the total available, were hitched to trains and reserved for Occupation personnel. Even though these cars might be unoccupied, they were off-limits to Japanese jammed into the rest of the train. Such problems led some disgruntled Japanese to look for scapegoats, and Sogo became a target.

Someone apparently wrote anonymously to U.S. forces charging that Sogo had mistreated Chinese prisoners of war, who had been forced to work in a coal mine near Izu. Sogo came under investigation as a suspected war criminal.

Sogo had indeed visited the mine where some 200 of his student volunteers were working alongside a similar number of Korean contract laborers and Chinese prisoners. He found the Chinese were particularly unhappy about their food which, aside from being insufficient, was totally unlike their regular diet, which included more oil and fat than the Japanese were accustomed to. Cooking oil and meat were strictly rationed. There was no way to get better rations for the Chinese without tapping the black market, which Sogo did without hesitation. He managed to locate some black market fish and pork, had it taken to an isolated mountainside where the cooking odors wouldn't be noticed by area residents, and gave the Chinese at least one decent meal.

Chinese officials attached to the Occupation headquarters came to Sogo's aid when they heard of the investigation. One of them told Sogo that he knew of Sogo's efforts to end the fighting in China, that he had heard of Sogo's kindness toward the

Sogo (center) with Transportation Minister Takeo Miki (left) at the press conference in 1955 announcing he had accepted presidency of the Japanese National Railways (JNR).

Accompanied by her physician, Dr. Masahiko Narasaki, Kiku, who suffered severe asthma attacks, and Sogo were photographed on a picnic outing to the Tokyo suburbs in 1957.

The last photo of Kiku and Sogo together, taken July 3, 1958, by their son Shinsaku at their Tokyo home. She died three weeks later.

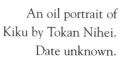
An oil portrait of
Kiku by Tokan Nihei.
Date unknown.

Sogo, with fan, at the press conference on July 7, 1958, announcing the Survey Committee's decision to support the Bullet Train project. Sogo was then 74 years old.

Sogo, at the tomb of his mentor Shinpei Goto, reports on the cabinet's decision to proceed with the Bullet Train.

Sogo, at the ground-breaking ceremony for the Bullet Train project, swung his hoe so vigorously that the head flew off. *Courtesy of The Railway Technical Research Institute, Tokyo.*

Poem and calligraphy by Sogo. Roughly translated, it says: "Under the bright sun, hammers sound loudly to proudly announce the beginning of construction on the Bullet Train."

Sogo customarily took his work home with him. Eldest daughter
Michiko (far left) and granddaughter Tsugiko keep him company.

Sogo (right) with his good friend Kenzo Asahara, who was in the plot to overthrow
Prime Minister Tojo's government. Photo probably taken in the late 1950s.

Signing ceremony formalizing the World Bank loan to the Bullet Train project. Seated left to right: Japan's ambassador to the U.S., Koichiro Asakai; Sir William Iliff, vice president of the World Bank; Sogo. *Courtesy of the International Bank for Reconstruction and Development, Washington, D.C.*

LOAN NUMBER 281 JA

Loan Agreement

(New Tokaido Line Project)

BETWEEN

INTERNATIONAL BANK FOR RECONSTRUCTION
AND DEVELOPMENT

AND

JAPANESE NATIONAL RAILWAYS

DATED MAY 2, 1961

9

For the Bank:
International Bank for
    Reconstruction and Development
1818 H Street, N.W.
Washington 25, D. C.
United States of America

Alternative address for cablegrams and radiograms:
    Intbafrad
    Washington, D. C.

IN WITNESS WHEREOF, the parties hereto, acting through their representatives thereunto duly authorized, have caused this Loan Agreement to be signed in their respective names and delivered in the District of Columbia, United States of America, as of the day and year first above written.

INTERNATIONAL BANK FOR
    RECONSTRUCTION AND DEVELOPMENT

By _____
            Vice - President

JAPANESE NATIONAL RAILWAYS

By _____
            Authorized Representative

Top page and signature page of the World Bank loan agreement. *Courtesy of the International Bank for Reconstruction and Development, Washington, D.C.*

Prototype of the Bullet Train takes shape March 1962. Sogo, then 78 years old, is at the center. The tall man second from the right is Hideo Shima, the engineering wizard responsible for the technical side of the Bullet Train project.

U.S. Ambassador and Mrs.
Edwin O. Reischauer get an
explanation from Sogo during
a test run late in 1962.

In April 1963, the
Economic Commission
for Asia and the Far East
met to study the New
Tokaido Line (Bullet
Train) project.

Farewell party in May 1963 for Sogo, then 79 years old, after completing his second and final term as JNR president.

"Thank you" party for Sogo (left) with former Prime Minister Shigeru Yoshida in July 1963.

Sogo looks pensively at the Bullet Train after its first complete Tokyo-Osaka test run on August 24, 1964.

Official ceremony prior to send-off of the Bullet Train on its first official run.
Courtesy of Transportation News Co., Ltd.

Emperor Hirohito and Empress Nagako at the Bullet Train launching ceremony at
JNR headquarters.

On November 3, 1964, Sogo was decorated with the Grand Cordon of the Order of the Sacred Treasure. He commemorated the event by having his portrait taken with a painting of his late wife, Kiku.

On September 29, 1969, Sogo was named Honorary Citizen of Saijo City, and a bust was erected in his memory.

A memorial service was held for son Kosaku and wife Kiku on May 19, 1974. Participants signed a large card. Sogo was then 90.

Sogo read widely in retirement. Behind him is a portrait of his mentor, Shinpei Goto. *Courtesy of The Sankei Shimbun.*

Sogo with Yoshishige Abe, close friend since Ichiko School days.

Sogo (center) with two of his best friends, Nobutane Kiuchi (left) and Shigeharu Matsumoto. October 13, 1977.

Sogo, then 90, with his chief engineer, Hideo Shima. October 14, 1974.

Sogo, in wheelchair, celebrated his 96th birthday with members of his extended family. May 17, 1980.

Sleek Bullet Train speeding east of Okayama. Taken in 1989.
Courtesy of Transportation News Co., Ltd.

Commuters and long-distance travelers enjoy the convenience of the Bullet Train.
Courtesy of Transportation News Co., Ltd.

prisoners, and that Sogo had nothing to fear from the Americans. As it turned out, Sogo turned the tables on the young American officer who questioned him.

After explaining how he had fed the Chinese rather than mistreating them, Sogo said: "I spent quite a lot of time in China and Manchuria with what might be considered to be occupation forces, but never commandeered anyone's house at gunpoint. I always negotiated with the owner and either leased it or purchased it a reasonable price.

"But you Americans came suddenly into my home in Tokyo and ordered me to leave in five days, because it was needed for your officers. Do you think that is a fair way to do business? No, it is the action of a conqueror seizing the property of the conquered and totally unbecoming of you Americans.

"As for the Chinese, they had little to eat, and I took the risk of secretly giving them food I purchased on the black market. Chinese friends sent me letters of thanks. Yet you charge that I mistreated the Chinese. How can you, representing people who took my house, sit in judgment on me, the man who lost my house to you?"

The charges were dropped.

But not all Japanese were so fortunate. Some were found guilty of petty infractions during the war and removed from office or barred from responsible posts. At the same time government bureaucrats, who lacked initiative in any case, found their hands tied because permission from American Occupation officials was necessary for all but the most routine activities. The confusion and red tape stifled Japanese efforts to rebuild their economy. The government itself did not seem to have a vision for recovery. Many men denied an active role in the reconstruction of Japan organized informal "study groups" to discuss their country's future and draw up blueprints for achieving those goals. Sogo was one of them. He knew that with the destruction of Japanese factories, limited raw materials, and the loss of man-power at home and loss of markets on the Asian mainland, the nation would have to struggle to rebuild its economy.

For the time being, however, he had problems to solve in Kosai-kai. Foremost was lack of funds to carry out its programs. The nimble Sogo brain came up with a proposal for sharing the burden with the local branches of major banks. The branches would lend Kosai-kai the funds it needed to upgrade and stock its station platform shops. In turn the branch banks would collect each day's income from these shops, but remit the money to the central bank only every 10 days. Thus, the branch would have interest-free use of the money during that period. While it would appear only a small amount was involved in each store, that sum multiplied by many shops added up to a sum substantial enough for the bankers to accept the proposal.

Sogo, freed from routine matters, spent much of his time traveling over the railroad system, chatting with operators of the platform stores, listening to problems of retired employees. He took particular interest in a school for the retarded being run by Kosai-kai and helped set up an agricultural colony and after-care center for the patients.

On April 15, 1948, the day after he reached his 64th year, Sogo resigned as president of Kosai-kai. By the Japanese system of calculating age, he was a year old the day he was born and thus 65 years on his 64th birthday. "I must make way for younger people," he said as he stepped down.

He sold his Tokyo home and moved with Kiku to a rustic old house facing Sagami Bay near the foot of Mount Fuji, looking out over the restless blue Pacific, not far from the railroad station at Kozu, about 50 miles southwest of Tokyo. Kiku was a familiar sight as she trudged to the shops each day to buy fish and vegetables and tofu for Sogo's meals. There was time now for reading and thinking and visiting with old friends who came to call. But Sogo's mind was restless, and he continued to be active with what now would be called a "think tank," the Nihon Keizai Fukko Kyokai, which functioned as a volunteer Committee on Economic Reconstruction. Trade, financing Japan's reconstruction, and long-range plans for economic recovery came under its purview.

One project interested Sogo in particular. He heard a botany professor at Tokyo University had been experimenting with a strain of rice tolerant to cold temperatures. Rice flourishes in tropical and semi-tropical climates but not in the rugged valleys of northern Japan. If a hardy type could be developed, the supply of Japan's staple food would be increased substantially. Sogo persuaded friends in the Diet to subsidize experiments, and when they showed promise, his organization printed and distributed brochures promoting the hardier variety.

Sogo also kept in touch with the "old boys" in the railway system, often traveling with them to inspect the way the trains were being run. They noted shortcomings, like lack of water in the washrooms, dirty windows, excessively cold or overheated cars, inconsiderate conductors. Back home again he wrote voluminous letters reporting his findings to officials of Japanese National Railways (JNR), which became the new name for the Ministry of Railways in 1949. When he heard American military officers saying Japan as a defeated nation did not deserve the luxury of a modernized railroad system, he wrote letters of protest to Occupation officials.

Few if any of these letters ever received a reply. On one of his trips to Tokyo he visited JNR offices and asked a department chief if he had ever seen the letters Sogo had sent him.

"No, I don't think so," the man replied. "They must have been misplaced. I will check on it later."

Sogo replied: "No need to check. I have brought copies of all of my letters. I expect answers. If my criticism is unjustified, please explain where I am wrong. If my criticism is justified, please do something about improving the service."

Still there was no response. Later Sogo heard the department chief had sneered at his letters, saying: "The old man has too much time to complain. I don't have time to humor him."

Sogo took that to be an insult, not to him personally but to all who utilized the railway system. He still remembered the incident some years later when he was able to do something about the public's concerns.

有法子

CHAPTER 16

CHALLENGE

One day in the spring of 1954, Shinji Sogo was hurrying up
the stairway at Kozu station near his home to catch a train for
Tokyo when suddenly the scene in front of him did strange
things. The stairs became blurred. People in front of him were
simply shadows. Sogo groped for the railing. Someone guided
him back to his home. Kiku, thoroughly alarmed, hurried him to
the clinic for railway employees not far away.

Doctors found Sogo's blood pressure was fluctuating wildly,
causing changes in the angle of his astigmatism. Sogo was transferred to the Railway Hospital in Tokyo's Shinjuku district and
placed in the care of specialists. But even they were unable to

stabilize his blood pressure.

Sogo had been a sturdy farm boy but had acquired various ailments as he grew older, some of them perhaps the result of idiosyncrasies. During much of his later life, unmindful of warnings about cholesterol, he ate an omelet of two or three eggs with his toast every morning. He also enjoyed sweet potatoes, miso soup, grated radish flavored with soy sauce, and vinegared mackerel sushi. But he was allergic to shrimp, crab, and spinach and avoided them.

He had odd sleeping habits. The average person is said to turn over about 25 times during a night's sleep, but Sogo rarely shifted position. He wrapped himself in a quilt even on hot summer nights, and his sheets were soaked with sweat by morning. In sleep his pulse was irregular. He snored loudly but sometimes became silent abruptly, much to the alarm of his secretary sleeping in an adjoining room on the other side of a flimsy *shoji* screen.

Five months in the hospital brought about no significant change in his condition. Kiku, who under Japanese custom had been tending to his needs at the hospital and suffering herself from high blood pressure, was near exhaustion.

One day a physician friend named Tanihei Sakai visited Sogo. Sitting at Sogo's bedside, Dr. Sakai said:

"My friend, I have seen your medical records. The doctors seem to have done everything possible to control your blood pressure. There is nothing more the hospital can do for you. Your wife is not well and needs to be relieved. You are well enough to go home and relax, and that would be the best course of treatment for you.

"But the hospital administrators dare not tell you to leave. They would not feel it right to do that until you are fully recovered. It would be best for everyone if you insisted that you want to leave. You can act like a stubborn old man who simply wants to go home, and the administrators will agree to let you go. You can get regular checkups at the railway clinic near your home. My friend, take my advice."

A few days later Sogo left the hospital and returned to Kozu to complete his recuperation. He spent much time reading, mostly on politics and economics although occasionally he read translations of French novels. He turned on his television set only to get the news. Gradually, as his health improved, he took short trips or invited friends to his home. Sometimes he went to Osaka to see the Bunraku puppet plays and chat with Bungoro Yoshida, who, as director of the Bunraku Theater, was considered a living national treasure.

At his age Sogo could act the crotchety old man. He insisted on punctuality even though time meant little. If a visitor were late for an appointment, he could expect a rebuke. When Sogo made an appointment, he was likely to appear a half hour early although he rarely hurried. He awoke early and spent an hour washing, shaving, and having breakfast. Then he would disappear for a half hour into the lavatory. It took him another half hour to dress.

Sogo liked to have his underwear ironed. "You never know what's going to happen once I leave home," he said. His suits were unstylish and the trousers baggy. He was barely 5 feet 3 inches tall and had a figure that would challenge the best of tailors. Since ready-made suits were virtually unknown at the time, he had his clothes tailored at an inexpensive shop near his home in Hongo. He patronized the shop over the years, even after he could afford better, because he felt an obligation to continue supporting the owner. He liked ties with a splash of red in them. His handkerchiefs were specially dyed with a morning glory pattern, and he always carried two of them.

During his recovery period Japan suffered two major maritime disasters. Although Shinji Sogo had nothing to do with them, in a curious way they changed his life.

In September of 1954, a ship named the *Toya Maru* was sailing between Hakodate on Hokkaido Island and Aomori on Honshu, the mainland of Japan. It ran unexpectedly into a fierce storm. The *Toya Maru* was blown aground where it capsized with a death toll of 1,155. Two other ships sank in the same storm with another 275 deaths. About eight months later, in the spring of 1955, the *Shiun Maru*, an excursion ship operated by JNR, collided with a freighter also operated by the railway. Of the 168 passengers lost, more than 100 were elementary and junior high pupils on a school excursion.

This second tragedy, following so soon after the earlier disaster, shocked the nation. Accepting personal responsibility as was customary, National Railways' President Sonosuke Nagasaki resigned. None of the men suggested as Nagasaki's successor was quite right for a job that required leadership, some technical knowledge, and the ability to regain the public's confidence in the nation's railroad system. Someone who could rally employee morale and restructure and revitalize the organization was badly needed. These were difficult qualifications to meet, and the few possible candidates firmly refused the appointment.

Then Shinji Sogo's name came up. The recently installed Prime Minister Ichiro Hatoyama and Takeo Miki, minister of transportation and later a prime minister, approved of Sogo. An emissary was sent to Kozu to inform Sogo of the prime minister's wishes.

"Ridiculous," Sogo exclaimed when he was told the news. "Consider my age. Consider that I am not fully recovered from a long illness. Consider my lack of ability. Consider my less than brilliant record with the South Manchuria Railway."

Nonetheless, Sogo agreed to discuss the appointment with a second group of emissaries in a Tokyo teahouse. The men he met had prepared well. They reminded Sogo that he, a poor farmer's son, had said he owed a debt to society for the education he had received, and that he had joined the Railway Agency in order to serve the public. The National Railways, in a sense, is like your mother, and now it is in deep trouble, they said. You have an opportunity to save your mother from her problems, but you give silly excuses such as old age and ill health to avoid coming to her aid. What are you afraid of? If you possess any *Bushido*, the Japanese warrior spirit, you would not be afraid to die for a good cause.

It was just the sort of taunt that moved men of the Meiji Era. They could not stand being accused of cowardice, lacking the *Bushido* spirit, or ignoring the nation's needs in times of trouble. Late that very same afternoon, Sogo met Transportation Minister Miki in a room at the Tokyo Station Hotel. Their discussion lasted only 40 minutes.

Miki told Sogo his job would be to rebuild discipline and morale among railway employees, to review the entire structure of JNR and define clearer lines of authority and responsibility, to restructure the financial system, and to take all necessary action to regain public confidence following the *Shiun Maru* disaster. It was a staggering agenda but the sort of challenge that piqued his interest.

Now Sogo in turn asked that the National Railways be given greater independence from politics and politicians, that he as president have final authority on management decisions although he would seek the advice of government and political parties, and that the government would cease bowing to regional pressures and refuse to build unprofitable new lines.

The two men shook hands on the agreement, and Miki led Sogo out to meet the press which had been summoned hurriedly. Asked by a reporter why he had taken the position, Sogo replied:

"You know that I was hospitalized until recently and have not fully recovered. However, the National Railways is in difficulties. I have an obligation to help restore its reputation as the backbone of the Japanese economy. The railway was the starting point of my career, and now, if it is in my power to solve its problems, I am ready to dedicate the rest of my life to the effort." Then with bravado, he added: "I am ready to die on the tracks."

Next morning, after his appointment was confirmed by the cabinet, Sogo met with a delegation of JNR employees. He said the first priorities would be safe operations to regain public trust, to develop a spirit of teamwork among all workers, and to help reconstruct the nation's economy.

"I have answered the summons of the government in the same way that I would respond to an *aka gami* draft notice calling me to military service," he declared.

Railway workers responded enthusiastically, but the press was critical of what they considered to be Sogo's fatalistic attitude. Hideo Aragaki of the *Asahi Shimbun* wrote: "Appointment of Shinji Sogo is like bringing out an old locomotive from the railroad museum. The new president told us he was ready to die on the tracks. What a troubled society we live in."

The medical staff at the Railway Hospital was astonished at the news. They knew Sogo's health was precarious and had doubts that at age 71 he could stand up under the pressures of his new responsibilities. They read into his comments about being drafted and being prepared to die on the tracks as indication of Sogo's determination to serve even if it meant giving up his life.

Sogo's first important duty as president was to attend a memorial service for victims of the *Shiun Maru* disaster. It was held in Takamatsu City on Shikoku Island where most of the young victims had lived. When it became Sogo's turn to speak, he stepped forward and began: "Message of condolence." But he could say no more. His face was contorted in grief, and his hands trembled. Finally, he composed himself enough to read his apology for the grief the accident had caused and promised to do whatever he could for the aggrieved families.

The National Railways paid ¥300,000 to each victim's family, but the money was not as important as the government's gesture of sympathy. The families of students from Hiroshima who died in the shipwreck donated some of the compensation money to build a library. Railway employees contributed to the fund. Their union at its annual convention a short time later also held a memorial service.

Sogo's next order of business was to meet with union leaders to ask for cooperation in restructuring JNR. At their first meeting, Sogo explained why he had come out of retirement to accept the presidency, outlined his plans for reconstruction of the system, and asked for union cooperation.

The response was not what Sogo had hoped for. A union spokesman named Akira Iwai declared coldly: "Your ideas are not so different from ours. We will watch you carefully to make sure you keep your promise."

"You disappoint me," Sogo retorted loudly. "National Railways is facing an extremely difficult time, and reconstruction will not be easy. No one else wanted to take the presidency so I felt obliged to accept the responsibility. The reality is that JNR has little independence, because the government and the political parties want to control us. Because I am not a politician, I have little power. Because ours is a government agency and not a private business enterprise, I do not have funds necessary to carry out our mission.

"Despite these handicaps, I accepted the presidency because I believed National Railways 500,000 employees were as concerned about the organization's future as I was. Now you union members say you will watch me try to save our organization. You talk as though you are totally uninvolved. The reconstruction of JNR is YOUR problem, or more correctly, OUR problem," Sogo roared, pounding the table. "If you do not share responsibility for reviving JNR, my promises will remain just words."

Iwai was stunned. "You are right, President Sogo," he said quickly. "I apologize. You have our pledge of cooperation."

Sogo had been confident he could deal with the unions, which during the U.S. Occupation had become increasingly militant under leftist leadership. He took the position that employees and employers had similar interests and difficulties could be overcome if they talked in a straightforward manner. He had not anticipated the growth of leftist philosophy that held that management and labor were in perpetual conflict. After his clash with Iwai, he felt he had reached an understanding with labor. But it was only the beginning of his problems with the union. Two decades later, one of his aides, Gohei Tani, wrote in his memoirs:

"President Sogo proposed including union leaders in the highest decision-making committee of National Railways and let them share responsibilities. We were perplexed by his progressive idea. Even if we told him that his idea was not legal, he would not listen. We thought that the best way to persuade him was to get academicians to tell him that his idea would not work. We invited Kazuo Okouchi and Teruhisa Ishii to talk with the president. They reached the conclusion that even if union leaders might like the idea of participating in decision-making, there would be no guarantee that they would take fair responsibility. In fact, it was not union policy to cooperate with management. After that he did not bring up the subject again."

Realizing his inability to deal with the unions, Sogo turned over labor relations to two of his assistants. Still, he was sensitive to public reaction. Remembering how his letters to National Railways had been ignored before he became president, he ordered all communications from the public to be answered promptly. When letters were addressed to the president, he replied personally, often working late at night to respond. But even that effort was ridiculed in *Kokutetsu*, a book written by left-leaning Professor Fujitaro Oshima. One passage read:

"After Sogo became president, he ordered employees to respond to all letters. Some workers have to work overtime to answer many stupid letters. Tokyo Station is said to have an assistant stationmaster just to answer letters. Does the president really think that he can avoid strong public criticism against JNR just by answering letters?"

Sogo rushed to complain to the publisher who he had known since boyhood. But the publisher, Shigeo Iwanami, was dead, and his son, the company's new owner, ignored Sogo's protests. Sogo then ordered JNR's new information department to produce a book setting forth a different picture of what he was trying to do. Titled *Japan's Economy and the National Railways*, it was not published until six years later.

Sogo's efforts at internal public relations were similarly handicapped. When he wrote a letter to union members underscoring the need for good human relations in reconstructing National Railways, leaders of some unions refused to circulate it among their members.

The depth of Sogo's dedication to his job, and particularly to his dream of building a standard-gauge trunk line between Tokyo and Osaka, and the realization of his mortality are evident in three messages to "Ones I Love" left in a drawer of his desk before he undertook trips abroad. Even in the 1950s, such travel was considered hazardous with no reassurance that one would return. Apparently he wanted to record his thoughts to be read if he died while overseas. The first was written August 1956, two years before Kiku's death, when he traveled for a month and a half to the United States and Europe. Kiku died in 1958.

Early in 1961, when Sogo was preparing to go to the U.S. to meet with officials of the World Bank, he wrote his second message.

His moving third testament, titled "My Last Message to Ones I Love," was composed late in 1961 on the eve of a trip to attend conferences of railroad industry leaders in India and Europe. A rough translation follows:

"Some people are trying to stop me from going abroad. I appreciate their concern very much. However, I have passed the age of 70, and there is nothing more honorable for me than to dedicate what remains of my life to the nation I love.

"I know no way to serve my country other than to work for the National Railways. If something extraordinary should happen to me during my overseas trip, I will feel honored to have finished my life while working.

"It has been a dream of our leaders since the Meiji Era for the nation to build a standard-gauge Tokaido Trunk Line. Making this dream a reality is my responsibility to the people who came before us. If Heaven allows me to accomplish this goal, I thank with deepest love the Supreme Being who enabled me to complete the task."

Fortunately for Japan, Sogo returned from his month-long trip with health no worse than before and brimming with new ideas and enthusiasm.

有法子

CHAPTER 17

BATTLE OF GAUGES

The Japan that confronted Shinji Sogo when he took over
JNR in 1955 was both challenging and confusing. The war had
ended formally on the signing of a peace treaty with the Allied
powers in San Francisco in September of 1951. The military governors of the Occupation went home to the United
States, and Japan once more became an independent
nation. The uncertainty, confusion, and hunger of the immediate postwar years at last had been overcome. Reconstruction
of the bomb-ruined cities was well under way. The Korean War
(June 26, 1950, to July 27, 1953) had been an economic shot in
the arm. American planes, trucks, and tanks were brought back

to Japan for repair and rebuilding by Japanese technicians. U.S. naval vessels sailed into Japanese ports for refitting and resupply. U.S. fighter planes from bases in Kyushu and bombers in Okinawa flew daily missions over Korea. Thousands of U.S. servicemen from the battlefront came back to Japan on leave with a great appetite for beer, women, and souvenirs.

Meanwhile, rebuilt Japanese factories had begun to churn out textiles, chinaware, toys, compact 35 mm. cameras better than those that renown German craftsmen were producing, and remarkable little battery-powered radios, no larger than a pack of cigarettes, using an American invention called transistors.

Machine tools, construction materials, home furnishings, and paper products were in great demand. Shipyards were requiring more and more steel from modernized Japanese mills to build fleets of freighters and tankers.

Business was booming, although by international standards Japan was still a third-rate nation. The gross national product was only one-fifteenth that of the United States and half of West Germany's. About 40 percent of the workforce was still involved in agriculture and fisheries industries and only 20 percent in manufacturing. Yet all signs indicated Japan's economy would continue to grow and grow and grow.

In the absence of a national highway system, Japan's rail transportation lines, which hadn't fully recovered from wartime devastation, were being utilized to the limit to meet demands of the booming economy. Yet there was widespread reluctance, even within the National Railways' hierarchy, to commit heavily to improvement and expansion. Trains were seen as a declining mode of transportation. The future of moving people and freight appeared to be in other directions. One had only to look to the United States and Europe to see that the most advanced nations were neglecting their rail systems in favor of highway and air traffic.

In Japan, mass production of motor vehicles had begun, and plans had been announced for building the nation's first four-lane highway to link Tokyo with Osaka and Kobe. In 1951 the government-financed Japan Airlines began operations, offering swift service between Tokyo and Osaka, and private airlines were in the process of building a domestic network. Port facilities were being improved to expedite transfer of cargo by water from one part of Japan—no place in the country is more than 75 miles from the sea—to another. Many were convinced that the railroad system needed only minimal improvement for a limited time before it would go into rapid decline, and therefore spending large sums of money on it was unwise.

A five-year plan for JNR, drawn up in 1954 (a year before Sogo took over), recommended emphasis on replacement of outdated facilities, improving capacity in underdeveloped areas of the country, and modernizing power sources. Out of a budget of ¥598 billion, only ¥12 billion was allocated for upgrading the Tokaido Line linking Tokyo and Osaka. Work was under way to electrify the last segment of the Tokaido system, and it was reasoned that when that project was completed the line's capacity would be increased sufficiently to meet foreseeable needs. But traffic continued to grow under the pressure of the national economic boom. Even after electrification was completed in 1956, the tonnage of cargo and number of passengers overtaxed the system.

Obviously, the capacity had to be enlarged. The big issue was how it should be done with the least possible cost. Some politicians advocated building a second set of narrow-gauge tracks parallel to the first.

Sogo was among the few who were convinced railroads would remain Japan's primary mode of transportation. And he believed it made the most sense to build an entirely new standard-gauge system for the Tokaido, using the newest technology.

It would be called *Shinkansen*, whose literal meaning was simply "new trunk line."

The *Shinkansen* idea was not new. As early as 1907, Zenjiro Yasuda, founder of the huge Yasuda economic conglomerate, had plans for his group to build an electrified standard-gauge railroad that would shuttle trains between Tokyo and Osaka in six hours. For the government, the idea was too outlandish. The plan never received official approval on the grounds that national trunk lines were the responsibility of the government and that private entrepreneurs like Yasuda should operate only local lines.

The possibilities for a standard-gauge system in Japan were demonstrated in 1924, when direct rail service was opened between Pusan, at the southern tip of the Korean Peninsula, to Beijing in China. The trip took 38 hours, but it was far faster than travel by ship. The route went up the Korean Peninsula, crossed the Yalu River on a long steel bridge into Manchuria, then swung southwest through Manchuria and North China to Beijing. A logical next step would be to build a fast rail link between Tokyo and Shimonoseki, at the southern tip of Honshu Island, with passengers being ferried across the narrow Korean Straits between Shimonoseki and Pusan. The following year, a government feasibility survey supported the idea of a new double-track standard-gauge line and equipment that could reach speeds of 120 miles per hour. These trains would travel from Tokyo to Osaka in four and one-half hours, and from Tokyo to Shimonoseki in nine hours.

That seemed to be no more than an impossible dream. Nothing came of the proposal, although improvements on the Tokyo-Osaka Tokaido Line 10 years later enabled the express, named *Tsubame* ("Swallow"), to cover the 500 kilometers (about 300 miles) in eight hours.

Finally, in 1940 the government became earnest about a

Shinkansen, although there was no agreement as to the shape it would take or the technology. A total of ¥556 million was budgeted for the project, with ¥6 million appropriated the first year to conduct another survey and begin purchases of some property needed no matter what the final decision would be. Some young engineers who had recently returned from study trips abroad were assigned to design passenger and freight cars that could be operated at a top speed of 120 miles per hour.

One of the major barriers on the route from Tokyo to Osaka was a range of mountains that reached almost to the sea. The original right-of-way had avoided the mountains by making its way along the picturesque seashore. If a tunnel could be driven through the mountains, substituting utility for scenery, the route could be shortened considerably. The Tanna Tunnel Project was started shortly after World War I and finally completed in 1934, at great cost and 16 years of effort.

A second Tanna Tunnel, to be called the Shin-Tanna, would be required for *Shinkansen*. The Ministry of War, which reviewed the plans, specified only that the second tunnel be far enough from the original to reduce potential damage from aerial bombing in case of war. Ground was broken in 1942, long before *Shinkansen* plans had been firmed up, because tunneling was expected to take a long time. Within a year shortages of manpower and materials forced shutdown of the project. The 4,000 constructions workers were reassigned to building underground air-raid shelters.

After taking over the presidency, Sogo lost no time in tackling the *Shinkansen* project. He realized it would be a staggeringly difficult undertaking without even considering the engineering problems. First, the idea would have to be sold to the public but, more specifically, to the Diet, which would have to approve the idea and appropriate start-up funds. After that the system would have to be engineered from the ground up and the technology developed, enabling trains to run as fast as 120 miles per hour. Finally, financing had to be arranged. Sogo was anxious to launch the project as quickly as possible, but he was too wise not to understand that first he had to establish a pro-*Shinkansen* consensus within both JNR and the public. At times it appeared that would be the most difficult part of the project.

Before launching his campaign, he needed even more facts and figures. He assigned a team of young engineers to begin yet another informal, preliminary feasibility study. One of them said later:

"We had just finished a project reviewing railway fares when we received orders to work on a proposed standard-gauge *Shinkansen* line. Why would they want still another survey? At first we thought Mr. Sogo was simply a stubborn old man pursuing a fantasy, but one of our senior engineers told us he was really determined to build the system. Well, that made it more interesting. We knew some of the senior employees in our office would be unhappy if they found us working on a standard-gauge plan, so members of our team began to take our work home, studying technological reports about what was going on in the U.S. and France, and making engineering calculations.

"The paper that really inspired us was an essay by Tadanao Miki, who had designed the very successful Ginga fighter plane for the navy during the war. He wrote that technically it was possible to design a narrow-gauge train to run between Tokyo and Osaka in 4 hours and 45 minutes. Using his data, we figured that a standard-gauge train could be designed to cover the same distance in 2 hours and 40 minutes, and the new system could be built at less cost than rebuilding the narrow-gauge system.

"Before the report could be delivered to Sogo it had to be approved by a senior committee. We knew we might be in trouble for writing such a report. We also knew that sometimes, when they were distracted, the senior committee members didn't pay much attention to what they were doing. We presented the report at the first meeting after the New Year holiday in 1956, when the committee members had a lot of other things on their minds. They approved the report with almost no discussion."

That same month Sogo called in his executive vice president, Hirohiko Tenbo, and asked for an official survey for a *Shinkansen* using international standard-gauge tracks.

"He did not take me seriously," Sogo said some time later. "Tenbo neither opposed me nor supported me. He thought to himself: 'This is just an old man's dream. Let him enjoy his dream. We are too busy for such nonsense.' "

Tenbo communicated his attitude to the senior engineers. What they produced was a compilation of old data assembled over the years. Angrily, Sogo confronted Matsutaro Fujii, National Railways' executive vice president and chief engineer, who had supervised the report.

Abandoning the delicate language the Japanese usually use in confrontations, Sogo said: "Mr. Fujii, for my executive vice president and chief engineer it is imperative that I have someone with a broader outlook than you have."

"On that, I agree with you," Fujii replied sarcastically.

"Then I must ask you to please step down," Sogo said icily.

"I wish you well in your search for someone to replace me."

Fuji accepted a transfer to the position of National Railways' executive director of construction, and Sogo set out to find a new right-hand man.

The person he had in mind was Hideo Shima, son of a former railway executive named Yasujiro Shima who was called "The Father of the Steam Locomotive" in Japan. The younger Shima was born in 1901, had graduated from Tokyo Imperial University with a major in technological studies, and had joined the railway as an engineer in 1928. He had demonstrated both engineering and human skills and moved up the ranks. He headed the teams that designed several outstanding locomotives and was responsible for construction of the highly successful Shonan electric train line between Tokyo and Numazu. In 1951, following a collision in which more than 100 passengers had been burned to death, Shima resigned in a symbolic acceptance of responsibility. In reality, it was unnecessary for Shima to leave, since National Railways President Yukio Kagayama and an executive director had already resigned. Shima accepted an executive position at Sumitomo Metal Industries.

Informally, Sogo sounded out Shima's interest in returning to JNR as director of technology and got a firmly negative reaction. Sogo then went to Osaka to call on Juichi Hirota, president of Sumitomo Metal Industries. He outlined his plans for JNR, explained why he needed Shima on his team, and asked that Shima be released from his commitment to Sumitomo Metal Industries.

Years later Shima wrote: "One day President Hirota asked me to come to his office. He told me that Mr. Sogo, president of National Railways, wanted me as his chief of technology. He went on to say that Mr. Sogo had asked him to persuade me to take the position. President Hirota said he would not stand in the way of what looked like a good opportunity and said the decision was mine.

"I reminded President Hirota that I once had worked for JNR, and that any plant transplanted to different pots many times does not grow well. I said I had known Mr. Sogo for a long time and would like to help him, but had no intention of returning to National Railways.

"Mr. Sogo was not discouraged. With President Hirota's permission, he came to me directly. He told me of his plans, and why he wanted my assistance. It was an exciting challenge technologically but also because there was no assurance that the project would even be approved. Finally, I agreed to work for him."

The two men had contrasting styles. In his later years Sogo was quick and forceful to the point of being bombastic in expressing his opinion. Shima was quiet. In group discussions he would listen without comment until a consensus seemed to be nearing his own ideas. Then he would feed hints into the discussion and deftly steer the decision around to his point of view.

Sogo wanted to make Shima an executive vice president as well as chief engineer. The table of organization called for only one executive vice president, and the bureaucrats refused to authorize the title for Shima. Sogo got around that by providing Shima with an office as large as the executive vice president's. When Shima's nameplate, designating his place at a board meeting, turned out to be smaller than the one for the executive vice president, Sogo threw it to the floor and ordered one of a more suitable size.

It was during this period that Sogo earned the nickname "Old Man Thunder" for his sudden displays of temper. The Japanese have a saying that the world's most frightening things are earthquakes, thunder, fire, and father, in that order. Fathers were to be feared and respected, and Sogo was National Railways' thundering father figure. A railways executive recalls that people of Sogo's era had a special skill in scolding as an educational tool, and Sogo was an expert.

One of his secretaries, Kenko Misaka, says: "Mr. Sogo was a typical Meiji Era man. When he was angry, he roared like a lion. Everyone in our department worked together in a large room without walls or partitions. When Mr. Sogo scolded me, his voice was so loud that even people in other parts of the room stood up at attention. When he was angry it was truly impressive, but he was fair and usually he had good reason to be upset."

He was no bully who terrorized underlings without purpose.

His employees knew that when he upbraided someone it was to underscore a lesson so that the same error would not be repeated.

One day a physician who visited Sogo to check his health said his blood pressure seemed to drop after he shouted at a subordinate. One of his aides jokingly asked: "Doctor, is there a medicine that will lower President Sogo's blood pressure without him yelling at us?"

Sogo grinned and retorted: "Doctor, is there any medicine that will make people smarter without needing to be yelled at?"

There was one memorable incident when Sogo was silent. The day after he had been scolded, a section chief died of a stroke. Sogo was speechless when he heard the news.

有法子

CHAPTER 18

DECISION TO GAMBLE

And yet more red tape. All the *Shinkansen* studies produced under Sogo's direction were still classified as preliminary reports. On the basis of these findings, the National Railways had to come up with a final recommendation that would be presented to the cabinet through the minister of transportation. Sogo named his new assistant, Hideo Shima, chairman of a committee of 45 made up of 23 higher executives, 20 section chiefs from the various departments, and two secretaries to discuss the issues once more and reach some kind of consensus. Sogo and the vice president were not members of the committee, and Shima had no vote.

Sogo addressed the committee's first meeting on May 19, 1954. He noted that JNR was committed to upgrading the Tokyo-Osaka line but acknowledged that no decision had been reached about the extent to which the facilities should be improved and whether narrow or standard gauge should be utilized. He was aware, he said, that the majority of senior members of the railways' hierarchy was committed to narrow gauge and asked for open minds as the earlier studies came under review.

"Unfortunately," Sogo said, "for too long the *Shinkansen* project has become nothing but a political issue, since National Railways is operated by the government rather than a private company. When the Seiyu Party was in power, it advocated building more new lines rather than improving existing routes. When the Kensei Party was in power, the priorities were reversed. Every time the cabinet changes, railway policies change. Whereas the track gauge, narrow or standard, is critical from a transportation viewpoint, the practical side of the problem seems to be ignored by the politicians. This committee must reach a decision.

"As you know, I believe strongly that a new standard-gauge line is the wisest way to go. I reject the thinking that we should simply improve the current narrow-gauge system and convert it to standard gauge later, when the economy improves. We must be forward-looking, taking the position that transportation will lead the economy, not follow it."

Sogo left no doubt about where he stood, but such outspoken leadership was not always appreciated by Japanese bureaucrats. There was little applause as he bowed and left the room at the end of his address.

Meanwhile, outside office hours, Sogo lobbied vigorously. He printed a little leaflet extolling the advantages of standard-gauge trains, carried a supply wherever he went, and passed them out liberally. He buttonholed politicians, bureaucrats, and business leaders. And he practiced what was called *youchi-asagake*, meaning he called on politicians and government officials at their homes early in the morning and late at night when it was difficult for them to avoid him.

In later years he recalled: "When I called in the morning at the home of some politician, he usually was still in bed. I told whoever answered the door that I would wait until the master awoke, and they usually let me in to sit down. When I went to a government minister's home at night, it was likely he hadn't returned yet from some meeting or dinner engagement. So I would ask to be permitted to wait until he came home."

Sogo found support from many influential men in government and other men destined to take important roles. The most significant exception was Ichiro Kono, a former agriculture minister (therefore with a large rural following) and powerful leader of the mislabeled Japan Liberal Party faction (later the dominant Liberal-Democratic Party) in the Diet. When Sogo called at his home one morning and asked for a brief meeting, he was told to wait outside. Presently Kono strode out and walked past Sogo with a curt "I have no time for you today." Sogo returned the next morning and received the same treatment.

Another friend of Sogo's, who was an influential member of Kono's faction, interceded, and finally he and Kono met. It turned out that Kono was less concerned with the configuration of the *Shinkansen* than whether the bureaucrats of National Railways could get the job done.

"I understand your plan," he told Sogo without committing himself, "but I doubt that an organization as rotten as JNR can cope with such a big project."

Sogo explained he had been hired to bring efficiency to JNR. "When the *Shinkansen* plan is finalized, I will have an organization in place to implement it," Sogo said. "What is important now is not how we will get the job done, but to determine whether your party understands *Shinkansen*'s importance as a national issue."

Sogo left encouraged but unconvinced that he had won Kono's support.

Meanwhile, the railways' internal committee scheduled four meetings at which various task forces would present their reports. The first of these was in July, nearly two months after the initial organizational session. The day following the meeting, members of the committee were surprised to find a newspaper interview quoting Sogo as saying National Railways would build a standard-gauge line putting Osaka within four hours of Tokyo. Speculation in the committee was that Sogo, frustrated by the committee's slow progress, had made his personal opinion appear like a done deal to stimulate a consensus.

The second meeting was held in September without noticeable progress, followed by one in January of 1957. Unlike earlier meetings when most committee members remained silent, this session was marked by heated discussion on the gauge to be adopted. Some suggested that further input from experts was needed before a decision could be reached. Others scoffed, asserting the committee had all the testimony it needed. Consensus still eluded them.

The final meeting was held on February 4, 1957. Sogo was brought in to see whether he might be able to expedite the discussion. They went over the same old arguments. The meeting ended without agreement. It appeared that everyone recognized the need to increase the capacity of the Tokyo-Osaka route, but the majority favored a cautious approach, improving and expanding the narrow-gauge system and converting to standard gauge at some appropriate time, perhaps as much as 20 years in the future. Sogo and Shima's engineers were strongly in favor of building an entirely new standard-gauge line as soon as possible. Most of the administrative staff ridiculed that proposal as the

toy of engineers. While Sogo fretted, the matter remained unre-
solved. Four months slipped by after the committee's final meeting, and still there was no report.

Then, unexpectedly, Sogo found support. On the 50th
anniversary of the founding of the Railway Technology Research
Institute, it released a study saying the Tokaido Line urgently
needed improvement and travel between Tokyo and Osaka in
three hours was possible using new technology. It was not what
was said, but who said it, that made the report significant.

Within a week, using the Technology Research Institute's
report as his chief reference, Sogo applied to the Ministry of
Transportation for formal authority to proceed with improving the
Tokaido Line. The application, in the convoluted form often
used in Japanese official documents (which still exasperates
foreigners), was more a request for official guidance from the
ministry rather than a proposal for a definite course of action.
It outlined the need for a double set of tracks along the entire
route, and said for the umpteenth time that the option was
between laying a second narrow-gauge track parallel to the
existing tracks, or starting afresh and building two parallel
standard-gauge tracks.

"Considering the importance of the decision, we would like
your input from the national point of view," the application said.

In effect, it appeared Sogo was yielding National Railways'
responsibility for making a decision. Actually he was anxious to
avoid further discord within JNR, which would result from taking a firm stand; at the same time he was confident the ministry
would support his standard-gauge position if he left it up
to his bosses.

But even this approach did not end the dissension. Under
Japanese business custom, key decisions must have unanimous
approval. That approval is attested to by each participant stamp-
ing the documents with his personal seal. Although by this time

there was no open opposition to Sogo's proposal at the top administrative level, there was plenty of passive resistance. It was, in effect, a sit-down strike. It took nearly three weeks to get the required 20 seals. One official, when presented with the documents, stamped them wordlessly and brushed the papers off his desk to the floor.

Sogo fidgeted impatiently, aware that the Railways Ministry was likely to take another interminable period before rendering its decision, even though the preliminary papers had been properly stamped. New committees would be appointed and hearings held, duplicating the work that had been done several times previously. Unfortunately, that was the way the government operated. There was one saving grace. Having made the application, National Railways was safe in pursuing detailed technical research.

In the spring of 1957, the *Asahi Shimbun* sponsored a railroad seminar, probably at Sogo's suggestion. Despite a torrential rain, more than 500 participants filled the hall not far from Tokyo Station. Shima's engineers gave highly favorable reports on the comfort, speed, and high degree of safety that would be provided by the standard-gauge system being developed in their laboratories.

The *Asahi* published an article that declared: "The technology is here!" and went on to describe the proposed *Shinkansen* train in glowing detail. It said the super express would race between Tokyo and Osaka in less than three hours at an average speed of 120 miles per hour. Rolling stock would be much lighter and streamlined to reduce wind resistance that consumed two-thirds of the horsepower required to run high-speed trains. The rails would be welded end to end so there were be no joints, and ties would be made of concrete for strength and durability. An automatic speed-control system had been developed for greater safety and efficiency, and passengers were assured the ride would be like travel over a paved highway in an expensive limousine. The tide was beginning to turn. Sogo glowed.

Shortly after the seminar Nobusuke Kishi became prime minister, and he appointed Sannojo Nakamura as transportation minister. Prepared for the worst, Sogo went to see Nakamura to make his plea once more for a standard-gauge *Shinkansen* line. Years later Sogo, recalling his first meeting with Nakamura, said: "He was very cooperative and encouraging. He said he would take responsibility for getting the cabinet to agree on my proposal. I could hardly believe my ears. Without him, I don't know how many more years the project would have been delayed."

Nakamura understood the need for public support. One of his first moves was to get the cabinet to approve a trunk line survey committee, made up largely of business leaders, to work with a committee from the National Railways in overseeing the *Shinkansen* project. Nakamura told Sogo: "From what I had heard, I was prepared for heated discussions when I introduced the proposal for an oversight committee. But everything went very smoothly. You must have done some intensive lobbying."

Sogo smiled to himself. His late-night, early-morning lobbying sessions with important individuals were paying off.

Among the members of the government's committee was the chairman of the Private Broadcasting Stations Association, the chairman of the Japan Productivity Center, the president of a major electric utility, the president of the semi-government Japan External Trade Organization, a college professor, the president of the Shibaura Institute of Technology, and representatives of the press. The committee chairman was an old friend, Kinmochi Okura, an advocate of standard gauge since the days when he worked with Sogo at the South Manchuria Railway. Okura by then was president of the Japan Travel Bureau, and later would be elected to the upper house of the Diet.

The committee's first meeting was held September 11, 1957. In his opening remarks Chairman Okura voiced his intention to work for the nation's benefit. Then turning to the transportation minister, he asked, "How determined are you to implement our findings?" Minister Nakamura minced no words: "I will be responsible for implementing the project to build the *Shinkansen.*"

Two subcommittees were formed, for technology and construction and for finance and management. Between September 11, 1957, and the following March 27, the full committee held eight meetings. Its draft report recommended a new double-track, standard-gauge *Shinkansen* to speed passengers between Tokyo and Osaka and upgrading of the old narrow-gauge system to move freight. It also recommended a construction budget of ¥194.8 billion, based on estimates submitted by Sogo.

Actually, the National Railways estimate had been substantially higher. How Sogo came to propose a much smaller budget is something of a mystery to this day. Since Sogo is now dead and his chief engineer, Shima, has not spoken, the full story may never be known. But it is possible to construct a fairly authentic scenario.

One day, the scenario would begin, Hideo Shima comes into Sogo's office with a proposed construction budget of more than ¥300 billion. Sogo studies the figures briefly, then barks: "The figure is too high. Cut the estimate in half and redo the budget."

Shima is astonished. "Sir," he says, "my estimates are realistic. It would be impossible to get the job done with half the money."

Sogo smiles and says gently, "What you must understand, my friend, is that not only would the Diet reject an appropriation for ¥300 billion, but those short-sighted politicians would demand that we go back to the less expensive plan to simply improve the narrow-gauge system. The standard-gauge project would be dead, perhaps forever, and our country would be denied the opportunity of a lifetime. If we permit our project to die, it would be a great disservice to our country. You and I must not let that happen."

Seeing the doubt and anxiety on Shima's face, Sogo continues, "Do not worry. The important thing is to get the job started, to advance it to the point where it cannot be abandoned. I will find ways and means to complete it. Supplementary appropriations are not impossible as the Diet reviews our progress. I know there will be bitter criticism, but how can it hurt an old man like me?"

Sogo smiles as he says, "I also have plans for private and foreign investment. I know that your figures are realistic. I know that I would be misleading the government in setting the budget at half the realistic estimate. But it is in the national interest."

That argument—that a seemingly imprudent decision was being made in the nation's interest—appears not infrequently in Japanese history, particularly in its military history to justify aggression. But in this case, at least, the gamble paid off. And there are unconfirmable reports that it was more than a gamble. Sogo, these reports say, had told supporters high in the government what he was about to do and had received their tacit promises of support. Whatever he may have been, Sogo was not rash, and that adds credence to this story.

Shima went back to his office shaking his head, partly in fear and partly in admiration of Sogo's bullheadedness.

The final report was delivered to the transportation minister on July 7, 1958. In addition to recommending that a standard-gauge system linking Tokyo and Osaka be built with all possible dispatch, it urged consideration for extending the line in both directions at a later stage. To get the project underway without further delay it recommended a construction budget of ¥172.5 billion, including ¥10 billion for rolling stock, for a total appropriation of ¥194.8 billion.

On December 19, 1958, the cabinet approved the report. That was the official go-ahead to build *Shinkansen*. There were no more red-tape barriers to be crossed. The only problems in the way of *Shinkansen* were technical ones. And the matter of raising more money when the appropriation ran out.

That evening, after he got the news, Sogo and his secretary drove to Aoyama Cemetery. There he visited the tombs of Shinpei Goto, Mitsugu Sengoku, Kaku Mori, and Tasuku Egi, old friends, supporters, and mentors, to report his success and thank them for their part in making it all possible.

有法子

CHAPTER 19

SAYONARA, KIKU

Six months before Shinji Sogo's great success in launching the *Shinkansen* project, the highlight of his career, he lost his wife, Kiku. She died on the morning of July 23, 1958, following an asthmatic attack. She was 71 years old and had been married for 50 years.

Despite her husband's prominence, Kiku's life had not been easy. Like a good Japanese wife of the time, she had catered to his every whim. Soon after her marriage in 1907, she had gone to live with her husband's family on rural Shikoku Island to be trained in the Sogo way of doing things while her husband continued his studies in Tokyo. In this role she was scarcely more than an uncomplaining servant girl. As his career progressed, Kiku remained in the background, rearing their children, looking after household matters, encouraging his successes, and commiserating with him in his defeats, accepting his stubbornness, quietly sharing his ideals.

Her eldest daughter, Michiko Kagayama, wrote: "When I was a young girl, because of my parents it was hard for me to think of married life as something filled with love and joy, and that a home was like heaven. Instead, I felt that a husband was trouble, and that a father was a person who always had a difficult job to do and was to be feared. When I saw my mother always obedient to my father, I felt sorry for her. She was the wife of a member of the elite, yet she was constantly burdened by household chores and spent most of her time taking care of her husband and children. She rarely talked about her days at the music college. Once she said, 'When I first heard the sound of a Western orchestra, I thought it was music from heaven.' I don't know what happened to her interest in music. At some point she completely stopped practicing, although there was an organ in our home."

Michiko remembers her mother as quiet and shy, and there were people who took advantage of her. Tradesmen sold her shoddy merchandise for which they charged high prices, but she did not complain. Michiko would become angry at her for allowing herself to be cheated. She would respond quietly, almost as though she were talking to herself, saying to Michiko: "You've never experienced real hardship. Real hardship is when someone is forced to cheat others." Only after Michiko grew up did she understand her mother's sympathy for those so desperate that they had to resort to dishonesty.

Sogo, full of vitality and ideas, kept himself busy with meetings and travel. But life changed in the immediate postwar years when the American Occupation requisitioned his home and he and Kiku moved to a small house in the peaceful little town of Kozu. There Sogo grew closer to his wife. It was not uncommon for him to take up unmanly chores like doing the marketing. He spent much time reading and thinking. Important passages in books he read were underlined in black and red ink, and comments, usually in strong disagreement, were scribbled in the margins. He contended that three hours of sleep each night were enough for anyone, although he often slept longer.

"During this period of isolation," Michiko wrote, "my mother was philosophical about accepting the turn of events. For a man, his wife's trust in a crisis is more helpful than words of encouragement. My mother was an obedient woman, but during hard times she demonstrated strength that was greater than my father's. Her presence strengthened him. How did they spend the lonely nights when the crashing of waves was so loud in their small beachside home? What did they talk about? Did they play cards together? I do not know, but I have no doubt that these were the closest moments the two of them spent together."

But Sogo returned to his old routine when, as president of National Railways, he and Kiku moved into the official residence in Tokyo. Every night he brought home a sheaf of documents to study. Often he read past midnight as Kiku sat by his side, refilling his teacup from time to time. Sometimes she seemed to nod off, but Sogo never told her to go to bed. And Kiku did not ask to be excused.

During times when Sogo had a chauffeur-driven car, he made it a habit to let Kiku enter before him. "It wasn't chivalry," Michiko says. "My father wanted to leave the car first, and he didn't want to stumble over her feet."

Despite Sogo's apparent self-centeredness, he took delight in playing games with his grandchildren. Often he pretended to cheat and took their protests good-naturedly. Sogo expressed special concern for a grandson who was slightly retarded. He helped the boy find a job. When the child's mother said she feared the boy's handicap might reflect poorly on his grandfather, Sogo scolded her, saying "Who should be more important to you, him or me?"

One day late in December of 1956, when the Sogo children and their families came home to celebrate the holidays, Kiku suffered a severe attack of asthma that affected her heart. She was never well after that. The plumpness in her cheeks disappeared, and often she was in pain.

Sogo cared for her tenderly. In a culture where business executives dine out almost every night as part of their responsibilities, Sogo had most of his dinners at home on a small table near Kiku's bedside. When she became too weak to feed herself, he helped her as if she were a child. He slept in the same room with Kiku, linking his wrist to hers by a cord so that she could tug on it and awaken him if she needed help.

Kiku's ashes were interred at Rishoji Temple in Tokyo's Suginami Ward. More than 3,000 persons, high government officials in formal wear and humble railroad workers in ill-fitting suits, attended the funeral ceremony at Aoyama Memorial Hall. The air was heavy with summer humidity and the sweet smoke of incense. When it came time for Sogo's part in the rites, he walked firmly to the altar where Kiku's black-draped portrait was displayed. He stared for a long time at the photograph before bowing his head in prayer. Then, looking up to the ceiling, he shouted a single anguished word—"*Sayonara!*"—and returned to his seat where he sat impassively during the rest of the service.

Customarily, friends of the deceased take monetary offerings to a Japanese funeral. The money is carefully wrapped in white paper, and there is a reception desk where such offerings are received and recorded so that proper acknowledgment can be made. In effect, this custom serves as a mutual insurance system. The contributions help pay funeral expenses, and at a future time the recipient families contribute in return to each donor's funeral.

But Sogo had announced beforehand that no offerings would be accepted. He was determined to pay for the ceremony himself, even if he had to borrow.

Sogo's reluctance to accept contributions is understandable. He had not forgotten his arrest and trial more than 30 years earlier on charges of taking bribes related to government purchasing contracts for reconstruction following the Great Tokyo Earthquake. He had been completely cleared then, but he wanted to avoid any suspicion of bribery related to the *Shinkansen* project.

The records show that funeral expenses were more than ¥1 million. A memorial service held a month later cost ¥75,000, and a third service in August cost ¥71,000. Sogo's salary as president of National Railways was ¥200,000 per month, and about half of it went for taxes. The funeral had cost Sogo nearly an entire year's income.

有法子

CHAPTER 20

CHARGING AHEAD

If there was a benefit to the long delay in getting the *Shinkansen* project started, it was that Hideo Shima and his engineers could work quietly, and largely out of the spotlight of publicity, on the myriad technical details while waiting for official approval. Sogo, the big boss, professed no knowledge of the technical and mechanical sides of running National Railways or building a new line. His job was to manage—to set policy, win political approval for it, and look for ways to finance it and make it work. Neither Sogo nor Shima could succeed without the other, and it is difficult to say whose responsibility was the more difficult.

They could work as a team, because each had absolute faith in the other's loyalty and abilities. Although no one doubted that Sogo was in charge, he gave the engineer virtually free rein to do what he thought best. Nonetheless, Sogo was known for his interest in details. When project managers needed to get his approval on matters they knew he would support only after long discussion, they would get Shima's endorsement first and let the old man know about it so they could avoid his "thunder."

Sogo's basic instruction to Shima was to utilize the best of current technology whenever possible, adapting it to his needs instead of attempting to develop costly, time-consuming, and possibly unworkable revolutionary ideas. After all, trains had been running successfully for more than a century.

Yet it was an entirely new system that Shima would put together, utilizing the wizardry of the new science of electronics as well the basic idea of iron wheels running on steel rails. One of the first decisions was to make the trains as light as possible, compatible with safety, to minimize wear and tear on the rails and conserve energy. Motive power would be delivered to each individual axle under every car instead of a huge locomotive pulling the entire train. *Shinkansen,* in effect, would be a string of self-powered cars traveling together, rather than being hauled by a single locomotive, and responding more quickly to the engineer's commands. The place the engineer would sit at the front of the train was to be the control center, not the source of power. As it turned out, the controls could be kept so compact that the engineer's compartment took up only the lead car's front third, with the other two-thirds available for seating passengers.

One of Shima's strengths was his ability to motivate others. He would paint a broad picture of what he had in mind, and soon his task force chiefs, made to feel that the entire project was their idea, would work with renewed vigor to come up with solutions.

Early on in the debate over motive power for *Shinkansen* trains, studies showed that one steam locomotive costing ¥36 million could produce 2,000 horsepower. By contrast, one of the newly developed diesel locomotives, while more flexible, would cost ¥60 million and produce only 1,000 horsepower. Despite this differential, Sogo wanted to switch from steam to the more versatile diesel for freight locomotives. He acknowledged that modernization would be costly, but he reasoned that on the other hand Japan could mass produce and export diesel locomotives and bring down their unit cost. *Shinkansen* itself would be a completely electrified system.

Rather than spending his limited funds to build *Shinkansen* cars, Sogo offered private manufacturers an opportunity to take part in the project. He asked them to construct the cars, then lease them to JNR for five years with an option to purchase. The manufacturers were happy to get the business. But they ran into a stumbling block when a bureaucratic bean-counter protested that the idea was illegal because the national budget was drawn up on a yearly basis and made no provisions for long-term contracts.

Once more Sogo demonstrated his impatience with red tape. "If you insist on calling my proposal illegal," Sogo thundered at a trembling bureaucrat, "then I am going to take illegal action, and you wouldn't want that, would you? Now go out and find some way to negotiate with the Ministry of Finance to implement this plan." Between 1955 and 1958 contracts worth ¥40 billion were placed with private car manufacturing companies. But before the contracts could be completed, the government, in one of its periodic economizing moods, slashed Sogo's overall budget by 10 percent. Angry but determined, he explained the problem to the manufacturers and insisted on and received a reluctant 10 percent price reduction.

To mollify the manufacturers Sogo organized a railway

conference in Tokyo for various Asian nations. The ostensible purpose was to exchange information, but Sogo used the gathering to showcase Japanese equipment. Before they went home, representatives of many nations agreed to buy Japanese products.

Toshiji Yoshitsugu, president of the Tokyu Car Corporation, said later: "Mr. Sogo didn't ask. He simply notified us we were to cut our prices by 10 percent. I thought him a terrible man, but then he gave us a great opportunity to export our products, and we made a nice profit."

"The whole idea worked beautifully," Sogo said some years later. "I didn't have to worry about the cost of depreciation on rolling stock and was able to divert to construction the money I didn't have to spend for capital purchases."

Sogo also turned to the private sector for electric power. From the earliest days National Railways had produced its own electricity. But building the facilities to generate enough power for *Shinkansen*'s anticipated needs was a dauntingly expensive project. He put it bluntly to leaders of the generating industry.

"We have too many projects under way, and not enough capital to develop the power we will need," he explained. "I offer you a large and steady market, if you will develop a reliable and abundant supply of electrical power at reasonable cost." The executives agreed readily to accept the opportunity and organized the Federation of Electric Power Companies to build and run the necessary facilities.

The pressure on Sogo as president of JNR came from many directions. Soon after he assumed the presidency Sogo was visited by an old acquaintance, Keita Goto, a former transportation minister who had become president of the Tokyu Corporate Empire with extensive interests in real estate.

After some small talk, Goto reminded Sogo that under a recently passed bill National Railways was authorized to build a line linking the cities of Ito and Shimoda on the Izu Peninsula south of Tokyo. "We would appreciate it very much," Goto said, "if you can build the line as soon as possible. It would be very helpful in Tokyu's plans to develop the Izu area."

Sogo turned livid. "It's an outrage that you should ask that," he retorted loudly. "What you want JNR to do is arrange our priorities to make profits for the Tokyu group. That is not the way I run my organization."

Sogo's dislike of Goto's tactics spilled over into another incident not affecting National Railways directly. One day a friend, Shikazo Abe, told him he was having difficulty fighting off a real estate takeover bid by Goto. Some years earlier, Abe had come to Sogo to ask his advice about a proposal to buy a swampy area called Hyotan Pond in the Asakusa area of Tokyo, put up an office building, reconstruct the huge Kannon Temple damaged in the war, and develop the grounds around it into a shopping and entertainment center. Sogo urged him to take on the project, reasoning that the postwar restoration of Tokyo would not be complete without redeveloping the Asakusa district. Abe then asked Sogo to take the largely honorary title of chairman of the development company. Sogo, who was unemployed at the time, agreed. But a year or so later, when Sogo was nominated as president of JNR, he resigned the Hyotan Pond chairmanship to avoid any conflict of interests. Now Goto was trying to take over the Hyotan Pond project.

Sogo listened intently as Abe told him of his problems. After a short while, Sogo summoned his secretary and told him to cancel a director's meeting.

"I have a stomach ache," Sogo said. "I am going to the hospital. Abe, I want you to come with me."

Abe saw no reason to accompany Sogo, but yielded to his insistence. Instead of the hospital, Sogo instructed his driver to take them to Tokyu's executive offices. Sogo, with Abe following, stopped outside Goto's door and shouted, "Goto, come out."

Everyone in the office stood up in alarm and bewilderment at this un-Japanese behavior. Goto stuck his head out the door. "Sogo, if you want to talk, don't disturb the office," he said. "Come in."

Once inside, Sogo simmered down. "*Goto-kun*," he said quietly, using the honorific title commonly employed by men addressing equals, "you have been causing our friend Abe much trouble. Do you really think it is fair to take over his project against his wishes? I want you to think about what will happen to Abe and his plans if you insist on having your way." Eventually Goto dropped his takeover campaign.

In its earlier years National Railways extended its holdings and interests well beyond running the government railroad system. These operations included a textile plant for weaving cloth for uniforms, timber processing for railroad ties, hospitals and medical clinics for employees, special schools for the children of railroad workers, and coal mines. As often happens, wages paid in these operations became higher than in private companies, and the government decided some of them should be privatized.

At the top of the list was the Shime coal mines, not far from Hakata in Kyushu. They had been managed by the navy as a source of fuel since 1888. In 1945 the mines were transferred to the Ministry of Transportation with more than 3,200 employees being moved to the government payroll. Shime was the ninth largest among some 500 coal mines in Kyushu, producing about 500,000 tons annually. But as the railways switched more and more of its locomotives from steam to diesel and electricity, the need for coal fell drastically.

Early in 1958 an outside committee named to study the problem recommended that JNR turn over management of the mines to the private sector with the Mitsui, Mitsubishi, and Sumitomo conglomerates being invited to submit bids. Sogo thought that was a good idea. The Socialist members of the Diet and Railway Workers' Union opposed it. One of their complaints was that committee members had never even visited the mine and didn't know anything about the problem.

Inevitably the press took sides without, as often happens, any real effort at investigation. One local newspaper published without attribution a report that Sogo had received ¥60 million from a mining company to give it control of the Shime mine, and that he had used the bribe to pay off the debts of another company in which he was involved. A second unconfirmed report said Mitsubishi had arranged to buy the mines even though competitive bidding had not started. One evening newspaper published a photograph purporting to show Sogo receiving a bribe.

Sogo was furious. The *Tokyo Shimbun* published an article that both supported and attacked Sogo. He was quoted as saying, "I have never accepted even one *sen* illegally in my 75 years of life." The article went on to say: "It is understandable that he is angry over false accusations. However, it does not help his reputation that he was the chairman of the Hyotan Pond company in Asakusa, even if it was for one year. Though the company never issued stock under his name, nor paid him, the fact that he was associated with a speculative development company does not add luster to his 75 years of life."

The criticism led the committee to schedule a visit to the mines. Sogo went along to lend support to the privatization decision. They were totally unprepared for the hostile reception organized by union leaders, Socialist politicians, Communist agitators, and mine workers. A crowd estimated at more than 8,000 blocked the way to the mine offices. Escorted by police, the visitors forced their way inside. An all-afternoon negotiating session led to an agreement that three union members would join the committee to review the privatization decision.

Four months later, when no agreement had been reached,

Mitsui, Mitsubishi, and Sumitomo announced they were no longer interested in taking over the mine. The changing energy picture, they said, made coal unattractive as an investment. Some years later JNR closed down the mine, and most of the employees were transferred to other jobs.

Sogo's problems were intensified by the fact that his four-year term as president of National Railways was nearing its end. Logic would dictate that with the *Shinkansen* project still at a critical stage, Sogo should be given a second term. However, there was no precedent for reappointment, and precedent is a powerful consideration in Japanese decisions. No president of JNR had ever completed even one term, most of them having resigned to take responsibility for allowing grievous errors or terrible accidents to occur. Sogo wanted to see the *Shinkansen* project through to completion, no matter what. He was backed by the giant Seibu conglomerate and opposed by the Tokyu group, which had not forgotten Sogo's tongue-lashings. Some of Shima's engineers petitioned Finance Minister Eisaku Sato, brother of Prime Minister Nobusuke Kishi, to reappoint Sogo. Labor leaders and Socialist members of the Diet demanded Sogo be replaced. Most of the major newspapers supported Sogo, charging that politicians were seeking a president they could control.

Perhaps it was Shigeru Yoshida, the elder statesman who as prime minister had rallied Japan's recovery during the Occupation years, that was most responsible for Sogo's appointment to a second term. One report had Yoshida writing to the president of the lower house making it clear that he would like to see Sogo reappointed. Another report had Yoshida telephoning Sato on Sogo's behalf. At any rate, Sato apparently had decided Sogo was his man two days before the official groundbreaking on April 20, 1959.

The ceremony was held at the Atami entrance to the Shin-

Tanna Tunnel, which had been started before World War II. Tunneling had progressed nearly a mile from each end when the work was suspended during the war. For more than 15 years, the bore had been maintained in anticipation of the work being restarted some day. The ceremony was held at the tunnel, because its completion was expected to be the most time-consuming part of the *Shinkansen* project. (Five years was the estimate for completion; it was completed in four.)

Red-and-white striped bunting was placed around the tunnel entrance and a Shinto shrine erected. Nearly 100 dignitaries and National Railways executives attended. Among them were Mamoru Nagano, the minister of transportation who wanted to replace Sogo, and Toshio Ogura, vice president of JNR who was Nagano's choice for new president.

There were the usual speeches, toasts, and a ceremonial groundbreaking. When it was Sogo's turn, someone handed him a small hoe painted gold. He raised it high over his head and, grunting "*Eiii*," drove it into the ground with such force that the decorative paper chrysanthemum pinned to his lapel flew off. Twice more he wielded the hoe with all his strength. On the third time, the head of the hoe flew off. After offering a toast with beer, Sogo delivered brief remarks:

"The ceremony is over. Thank you for taking part. This is the first step in construction of *Shinkansen*. It will be the world's best railroad system."

On the train back to Tokyo, one of Shima's engineers observed: "I have attended many groundbreaking ceremonies, and they all have been boring affairs. I have never seen anyone like President Sogo, who was so serious, so wrapped up in the significance of the event."

A reporter replied: "It was a surprise to see the hoe head fly off. What about Sogo's head? Will it fly off, too?"

On the following day Minister of Transportation Nagano

resigned, blaming health problems but hinting broadly that his proposal to replace Sogo with Ogura had been overruled.

One day later Ichiro Kono, Sogo's old nemesis, called on Prime Minister Kishi to voice his opposition to Sogo.

"An old man over 70 should not and cannot head National Railways just because he was good at getting along with the unions," Kono argued. "I have word that he asked the former Prime Minister Mr. Yoshida to support him for a second term, and also organized a movement among railroad workers to back him. How can a man like him be clean of any wrongdoing?"

The prime minister stood his ground. The cabinet approved a second term for Sogo, and he was appointed officially on May 12, 1959. A few months later Toshio Ogura, the vice president who had expected to succeed Sogo, resigned. Many Japanese now agree that if Sogo had not been retained, *Shinkansen* might never have been completed.

The *Shinkansen* route finally adopted ran 515 kilometers (roughly 320 miles) from a new station adjacent to the original one in downtown Tokyo to Shin-Osaka, a new station in downtown Osaka. Total land needs, including rights-of-way, were 11.8 million square meters (roughly 2,915 acres). Less than half was owned by JNR when the *Shinkansen* project was started. Purchasing the balance became a major task, especially after it became known they had selected a route and would have to acquire the property under any circumstance. Negotiations for the land did not begin in earnest until 1959. They were completed in January of 1964, only eight months before *Shinkansen*'s official opening.

National Railways started with 120 land-buyers but soon had to increase the staff because of difficulty in closing deals. The people in rural areas had to be cultivated in various, typically Japanese ways—with gifts of sweets and sake before beginning negotiations, attending local weddings and funerals as a demonstration of "sincerity" and interest in the community, and finally sitting down to long negotiating sessions with groups of landowners. Some landowners' emotional attachments to pieces of property had to be overcome. Others resented losing the long, narrow strips of land needed for the right-of-way. Still others were fearful of the thunder of trains racing past their homes many times daily. Newspapers reported that one landowner had hurriedly built a large home on land JNR wanted, to boost the value of the site. Another story said a landowner had put a price of ¥200,000 on an orange tree that would have to be cut down.

One stretch of the *Shinkansen* line ran parallel to Omi Railway Company tracks, blocking a beautiful view of the ocean, which Omi valued highly. To avoid further controversy, JNR paid ¥250 million in compensation, an item not included in cost estimates. Sogo ordered his staff to negotiate for the land as quickly as possible. "We must complete construction in the shortest possible time," he said. "I have no choice. I will take all the responsibility. Use your best judgment and do what you have to do. Go. Make decisions, sign contracts, pay money, buy land. National Railways will make back the money when *Shinkansen* is in operation."

A particularly sensitive problem arose in the routing west of Nagoya, a major port and manufacturing center. When the *Shinkansen* was first discussed before the war, it was planned to route it through the cities of Gifu and Ogaki on the way from Nagoya to Maibara. But postwar studies showed that by building a relative short tunnel, Gifu and Ogaki could be bypassed at a savings of 15 minutes of travel time and ¥15 to ¥20 billion in construction and land costs.

Gifu citizens were outraged at the prospect of being bypassed. Local politicians got into the controversy, which raged for months, until JNR agreed to build a new station at the city of Hashima.

And so it went, Sogo exhorting his people to speed completion of *Shinkansen* regardless of cost, while others, mainly politicians refusing to understand the impact the new train would have on the nation, continued to press parochial interests. Perhaps sensing his own mortality, and fearful that he might not live to see his project's completion, Sogo plunged ahead on his mission. He set up a new General Affairs Bureau under his personal supervision within JNR and gave it broad authority to cut red tape. There were some who likened National Railways to Japan's rogue Kwantung Army, which (ignoring the Tokyo government) had set its own policy of aggression in Manchuria and North China, a policy that had led eventually to World War II. It was an ironic comparison; few knew how Sogo had fought the Kwantung Army's influence on the mainland.

Criticism of Sogo was centered in the Diet among legislators intent on getting local rail service for their constituencies. To one committee, Sogo said "My mentor when I first joined the Railway Agency in my youth was the president, Shinpei Goto, who was also a medical doctor. He told me that in the human body the blood vessels are large close to the heart, and they are fed by a network of smaller veins and arteries that serve all parts of the body. The Tokaido area is the heart of the nation. Its population is 40 percent of the total. It also produces 60 percent of Japan's manufactured goods. It is the country's heart and requires a major transportation artery. As it continues to develop, there will be need for feeder veins and arteries, and we will build them. But the Tokaido Line must be developed first. I cannot divert funds and technical staff from Tokaido to build local lines, which are bound to be unprofitable for some time to come."

That made sense, but it was difficult to win over politicians who put their own constituencies above everything else.

有法子

CHAPTER 21

IN PURSUIT OF DOLLARS

As we have learned, the Japanese government's original appropriation of ¥194.8 billion for *Shinkansen* was a totally unrealistic figure. Hideo Shima's basic cost estimate was ¥300 billion, and it had been slashed at Shinji Sogo's insistence for somewhat devious reasons. If Sogo were worried about how he would find the funds necessary to complete the job, he didn't show it. In fact, he and Shima knew that no one could determine with any certainty what the final cost would be.

Shima's estimate was flawed, because it had been drawn up before many goals and standards had been established. While the budget was being debated, the precise Tokyo-Osaka route to be followed had not been determined. Even a slight deviation could affect land acquisition costs. The maximum speed to be achieved hadn't been agreed upon; the higher the speed, the more costly the construction. As it turned out, the Shin-Tanna Tunnel cost three times original estimates. Provision had been made for some 28 miles of costly elevated trackage; opposition to ground-level tracks in congested urban areas forced construction of more than 90 miles. Land costs proved to be five times greater than first estimated. The budget had taken inflation into consideration, but prices and wages rose much faster than anyone anticipated.

Salaries alone increased ¥20 billion each year, and the cost of steel, cement, and other materials kept pace.

Sogo could go back to the Diet for supplemental appropriations to cope with inflation, but he knew other sources of funding had to be found. The World Bank provided the answer.

Japan had joined the World Bank in 1952. Rebuilding Japan's national infrastructure required far more capital than the nation could scrape up, and the World Bank had been organized to invest in significant projects beyond the means of local funding organizations. Japan's electric industry was the first to borrow, followed by steelmakers and shipbuilders. The World Bank also had helped to finance construction of Japanese water systems and highways.

For National Railways, a World Bank loan would mean more than infusion of capital, without which the project might be crippled. Recognition by a world-class financial institution would give legitimacy to a project that, in some quarters of Japan, was still regarded as not quite proper. Furthermore, a World Bank loan would require the Tokyo government's signature as a guarantor and force future administrations to support the project to its completion.

Until 1957 World Bank regulations required borrowers to

purchase major construction materials only from countries that had invested in the bank. That regulation was changed in 1958 to open purchases to international bid, which meant Japanese firms could compete.

It was Eisaku Sato, minister of finance and longtime Sogo supporter, who first saw the World Bank as a possible financial backer for *Shinkansen*. Sato had attended the annual meeting of the International Monetary Fund in the United States in September of 1959. On the same trip he visited Martin M. Rosen, executive vice president of the International Finance Corporation, affiliated with the World Bank. They talked about the possibility of a $200 million loan for *Shinkansen*, and Sato invited Rosen to visit Japan.

At first the World Bank's project evaluators showed little enthusiasm for backing *Shinkansen*. They pointed out that the World Bank's mission was to contribute to the progress of developing countries, and therefore it might not be justified in helping to construct a technologically advanced railroad in a developed nation like Japan. Then the evaluators took a different tack: Was Japan competent to build the world's most sophisticated railway system? And finally, since railroads throughout the world were considered to be a declining industry, was it wise to invest in them instead of in motor highways?

Rosen went to Japan to seek answers to these and other questions. Sogo argued that, while railroads were declining in the United States and Europe, Japan was building a new railroad system from the ground up and suggested that that fact made Japan a developing nation.

Rosen then wanted to know how a developing country could build the world's most advanced rail system.

Sogo assured him new technology was being developed by teams of very competent engineers.

Rosen said he didn't mean to insult anyone, but he doubted

that Japan had that kind of expertise.

Sogo then took him to the Railway Technology Research Institute. Rosen found a huge, spotless laboratory where scores of Shima's engineers were working intently on literally thousands of individual problems whose solutions would be assembled into the *Shinkansen* system. Complex mathematical formulas were being devised and fed into computers for analysis. Model trains loaded with measuring instruments raced over miniature tracks and through long tunnels. In other buildings, wheels, springs, electric motors, and brakes were being tested for strength and stability.

Rosen was told that the heart of the *Shinkansen* system would be the transistorized Automatic Train Control (ATC), which would take over virtually all the driver's functions. Since human reactions would be too slow in an emergency for trains racing at 120 miles per hour, control over their movements would be placed with banks of computers in Tokyo, which would monitor the position and movement of every train in the system. The entire Tokyo-Osaka route would be divided into blocks, each with its own speed limit. For example, on an open stretch the highest allowable speed would be 130 miles per hour. On a curve or on approaching a station, electronic sensors would emit signals, and the electronic brains of ATC in Tokyo automatically would reduce power and speed, picking up again when the tracks ahead were straight and clear. The driver wouldn't have to worry about stopping his train at a station. ATC would do it for him precisely at a predetermined position along the track.

Rosen wasn't convinced all this would work. Sogo assured him that a 20-mile-long test track was being built outside Tokyo where the entire system would be put through a grueling series of trials.

Rosen was deeply impressed, but he was a banker, not an engineer. He invited Hideo Shima and some of his associates to come to Washington to explain the technology to World Bank experts. Their primary mission was to convince the specialists that while *Shinkansen* technology appeared to be experimental—which would have made the project ineligible for support—it was really an adaptation of well-established technology.

Satisfied at last, the World Bank agreed to send a multinational investigation team to Japan in May of 1960 to make a thorough technical evaluation. The team was headed by a Hollander and included a German and an American. Since France also was working on a super-train system and was a possible competitor, Japan asked that no French representative be included. The team spent more than a month studying *Shinkansen*'s economic and technical feasibility.

In December of 1960, the World Bank agreed to begin negotiating terms of a loan. On April 24, 1961, the World Bank granted a loan of $80 million, the third largest in the bank's history to that point and the largest loan to Japan. Sogo and his party flew to New York and took the train to Washington for the signing ceremony on May 2.

The night preceding the ceremony, Sogo's aide, Akira Kurata, handed him the text of a brief speech he was to make in English. Sogo studied it carefully, checking some of the words in his English-Japanese dictionary and adding pronunciation marks. He was unable to sleep when he went to bed and asked Kurata to get him a glass of sherry. But the hotel bar was closed, and no beverages were available.

The signing took place at 1 p.m. at the historic Mayflower Hotel. Sogo's remarks were brief but heartfelt. "Sir William," he said, addressing the vice president of the World Bank, "I am very happy to have reached the signing after long negotiations across the Pacific. This certainly provides a solid base for the *Shinkansen*. I promise that I will build a modern and efficient railway along the Tokaido within three years."

There was polite applause as Sogo, beaming, sat down. Afterward, the principals and some invited guests, numbering 30 in all, moved to the Mayflower's Chinese Room for lunch.

When they left the hotel Sogo suggested that the Japanese visit George Washington's tomb at Mt. Vernon. The day was pleasant, as May days in Washington usually are. Azalea blossoms were in full bloom. As they crossed the Potomac River, an aide said, "*Sosai* (Mr. President), this is the state of Virginia." But Sogo did not hear. He was fast asleep.

When he returned to Japan a few days later, Sogo once more visited the tombs of his mentors, Shinpei Goto and Mitsugu Sengoku. Bowing low, he clapped his hands together to attract the attention of the spirits and reported that his mission had been a success and that the completion of the *Shinkansen* project was assured.

The first remittance from the World Bank was received on July 22, 1961. The loan carried interest of 5.75 percent and was to be repaid in 20 years. No payment was required during the first three and a half years. Then, beginning in November of 1964, payments were to be made each May and November. Sogo lived to see the final installment paid on May 15, 1981.

The World Bank had loaned *Shinkansen* U.S. dollars, each of which was worth ¥360 at the current rate of exchange. Repayment was also in dollars, but during the period of the loan the value of the yen rose steadily. Eventually ¥260, then ¥240 became the equivalent of a dollar. The vagaries of foreign currency exchange rates benefited *Shinkansen* immensely.

有法子

CHAPTER 22

WELL DONE, SOGO-SAN

On June 23, 1962, a 20-mile section of standard-gauge *Shinkansen* test track was completed between the towns of Saginomiya and Ayase, not far from Tokyo. No one had ever seen railway tracks like it. All the ties were of prestressed concrete with rubber cushions between them and the rails. The concrete was more durable than wood, and the cushions dampened noise and shock. The rails were fastened to the ties by a shock-absorbing steel spring clip rather than spikes. The sections of rail were welded together, end to end in miles-long strips, so there would be no jolting, no familiar clickety-clack of wheels rolling over the joints. Planted outside the rails were scores of measuring and sensing devices to monitor pressures, weights, strains, wind velocity, vibrations, and noise. Perhaps one of the more remarkable tools was a track-inspection car designed to measure 16 types of strains, jolts, and pressures while running at high speed. It would be useful in maintaining the system.

The passenger cars were like nothing ever seen before in Japan. Because of the added width made possible with standard gauge, they were roomier than previous Japanese rail cars, comfortable and luxurious. First-class cars were designed with pairs of reclining seats on each side of a center aisle. The decor was richly textured gold-colored upholstery and stainless steel. For coach class, seating was three on one side, two on the other, with silver the decorating theme. Double-glazed glass windows were large and sealed in place.

Shinkansen in operation normally would have 16 cars, but the test trains were shorter. The standard configuration would be two first-class cars, a snack car, and the others would be coaches, although any combination was possible. Every car was heated and air-conditioned and, like airliners, sealed to protect passengers from sudden changes of pressure.

The exterior color scheme of ivory and blue, startlingly different from the traditional drab paint of railroad cars, exuded a sense of newness, speed, and excitement. "I want *Shinkansen* to complement the beauty of Mount Fuji," Sogo had told his designers. In fact, photographs of the long, low *Shinkansen* speeding past the towering profile of snow-clad Fuji became an important part of the new train's publicity campaign. With the rounded snout of the lead car, it did not take long for *Shinkansen* to be dubbed "Bullet Train."

When it was determined all was in order, the press and then the general public were invited on test runs. Reporters wrote glowing stories, marveling at the swift pickup and rides so smooth that even at two-mile-a-minute speeds water did not spill from tumblers filled to the brim. Tests continued through the fall and winter in all kinds of weather. On March 30, 1963, full power was turned on for the first time, and the Bullet Train was allowed to hit its top designated speed of 160 miles per hour.

There seemed to be little doubt that *Shinkansen* not only would work, but that it would be a monumental success. Sogo was as delighted as a small boy with a new toy. He rode the test train often, grinning happily, showing off its features to guests.

But even as the day neared for inaugurating Tokyo-Osaka *Shinkansen* service, two other events darkened the horizon.

The first was another ghastly railroad accident, a massive pileup outside Mikawashima Station, in which 160 passengers were killed and 325 seriously injured. The second was a renewal of complaints in the Diet about *Shinkansen* budget overruns.

The wreck revived fears about what would happen if *Shinkansen* crashed at high speed. The result would be like an airliner plunging into a hillside, it was contended, with no survivors and body parts scattered over the landscape. The braking system came under intense discussion. There were all manner of suggestions including one that the train should be equipped with emergency parachutes, like those that bring jet fighter aircraft to a quick stop on short runways, or even rockets with powerful reverse thrust. Some newspapers went so far as to prepare background stories to be filed away until a *Shinkansen* disaster did occur.

Shinkansen was designed with a double braking system. The first was the standard wheelbrake, in which brake pads are forced against the wheel by compressed air. The second, more difficult to understand, uses the mysterious power of electrical induction. As physicists discovered long ago, when the direction of direct current flowing through an electric motor is reversed with the flip of a switch, reversing the polarity of its magnets, they repel each other and instantly create a powerful drag. Thus, the motors would use electric energy to both propel and brake the train. In an emergency, the twin braking system could stop a train running at top speed in a little more than a mile, a remarkable feat considering the weight and momentum involved.

But the biggest safety factor was avoiding emergencies. There was not a single grade crossing the entire length of the new Tokaido Line. The Bullet Train had an unimpeded ground-level flight from terminal to terminal. And every train would be under the unsleeping electronic eyes of the Automatic Train Control System.

The Mikawashima disaster occurred about 9:40 p.m. on May 3, 1962. Investigation showed that the driver of a freight train, failing to heed a signal to stop, passed the station. When the train was quickly diverted into an emergency zone, the engine and first car derailed and fell atop an adjoining line. An electric train leaving the station crashed into the derailed engine and freight car, blocking still another set of rails. An incoming train slammed into the pileup, and its first four cars split open, spilling passengers like so many rag dolls.

Since May 3 was the beginning of a national holiday, Sogo was relaxing at an inn in Tateyama in Chiba Prefecture, just southwest of Tokyo. Although there was nothing improper about the president of National Railways taking a short vacation, a nervous public relations officer tried to avoid media criticism by indicating Sogo was attending a business meeting. The lie was soon uncovered. There was no train that night from Tateyama to Tokyo. Sogo was driven back to the city by car and reached his offices at 3 a.m., where he was brought up to date on the disaster.

Custom required Sogo to take complete responsibility for the accident. In fact, similar rail disasters had forced many of Sogo's predecessors to resign before their terms were completed.

But he was not ready for that kind of symbolic atonement. At daylight he and his aides hurried to the disaster scene. He visited some of the injured at hospitals and prayed for the dead at temples where the bodies had been taken. Then he began a round of excruciatingly difficult visits of apology to the homes of the victims. Many of them had lived in a congested laboring class area where tiny houses lined narrow streets. Bitter shouts met him at some homes: "National Railways killed my husband! What are we to do? No matter how many times you apologize, Sogo, it will not bring back the dead." Sogo told friends later that while it was painful to view the wreckage, it was infinitely more difficult to face the families of victims.

Almost before the dust settled, political enemies were calling for Sogo's resignation. Politicians who had been unable to persuade Sogo to build rail lines in their districts charged that he was so obsessed with *Shinkansen* that he was neglecting rail safety. Three years earlier, when Sogo was being considered for a second term as JNR's president, the more responsible segments of the press had supported him. This time few of them did. Friends urged Sogo to stick to his guns, arguing that he should not be held responsible for the wreck simply because he was president of the railroad. Sogo met with Noboru Saito, then the minister of transportation, and said he did not wish to resign while the *Shinkansen* project was unfinished, but would accept the government's decision.

Several years later Sogo told an interviewer, "After the Mikawashima disaster, many influential politicians demanded I should leave office. One told me it was a matter of conscience that I should give up my job. I replied my conscience was telling me to work even harder, and it would be irresponsible to quit. But I told him to get me fired if he thought it was the proper thing to do."

An investigation by the Ministry of Transportation found

the accident was the result of faulty employee performance and inadequate training and recommended better management of employees and improved maintenance of facilities. The report said nothing about the president's responsibility. Ultimately, it may have been the families of the victims who influenced the decision not to demand Sogo's resignation. They wanted Sogo to stay and work for more generous compensation for their losses. In any event, the minister of transportation told Sogo he need not resign.

But that did not stop the sniping. In August of that year a train on a rural line hit a truck at a crossing, killing the driver. Reporters found Sogo relaxing at an inn for National Railways' personnel. A photographer took a picture of him in an informal *yukata* robe, and it was published with a caption indicating the president felt no pain from the accident.

In February of 1963, with the *Shinkansen* project approaching completion, Sogo went to the Diet to ask for a supplementary appropriation of ¥95.4 billion which would bring the total government outlay to ¥292.6 billion. In some detail he explained the circumstances under which the original budget had been submitted and enumerated reasons for the overrun, such as inflation and incomplete data when the project was begun.

No doubt Sogo had been counting on the overwhelming success of the *Shinkansen* project to overcome misgivings about overspending. The budget committee, expressing understanding of Sogo's problems, approved the supplementary appropriation in March with minimal grumbling. Sogo and Shima congratulated each other.

But a month later, the press published sensational reports that Ministry of Finance auditors had discovered *Shinkansen*'s costs were still a stunning ¥87.4 billion in excess of government appropriations. The total bill was approaching ¥400 billion, more than double the estimate Sogo had submitted.

Why such a large shortfall should be uncovered so soon after the books were ready to be closed has never been adequately explained. In some societies, graft might be suspected. Although Sogo's name had been linked—wrongly, it turned out—with earlier financial improprieties, no one could seriously suspect one man could be responsible for anything on that scale. Sogo's personal frugality was widely recognized. And who would he need to bribe in the course of building *Shinkansen*, a project completely open to public scrutiny?

Several scenarios have been suggested. One blamed inept record-keeping on a project of unprecedented magnitude. There was also speculation at the time that the extent of the shortfall had been concealed from Sogo by bureaucrats in JNR opposed to his policies. Under this theory, the red-ink figures were leaked to the press through the Ministry of Finance by enemies who wanted to discredit Sogo and have him replaced before the triumphant ribbon-cutting that would symbolize *Shinkansen*'s success.

There was still another theory. It held that a faction headed by Shigenari Oishi, director general of the key General Affairs Bureau of National Railways, was so obsessed about protecting Sogo from criticism that Oishi manipulated the accounting to conceal the deficits even from Sogo. An investigation was begun. The paper trail led to Oishi's office. But he died before he could be questioned, and the mystery remains.

Whatever the reason for the shortfall, *Shinkansen*'s financial problem made it virtually certain that Sogo's second term as president of National Railways, which would expire May 19, 1963, would be his last. The bigger question was whether Sogo would resign before his term ended or wait until a successor was named. Reporters assigned to JNR took it for granted he would resign. When asked the question bluntly at a press conference,

Sogo replied that he would leave whenever the government asked him to do so. There were sympathizers in the lower house of the Diet who said Sogo should be kept on as honorary president and allowed to cut the ribbon at *Shinkansen's* inaugural run. Others contended Sogo had botched up National Railways so badly that he deserved no such honor.

Sogo was sincere when he said he would accept a third term but would not campaign for it. Many of his friends suspected that the real reason Sogo would have liked to stay was to complete the job of compensating families of the Mikawashima disaster and had nothing to do with ego. A month before his term was to end, Sogo asked his friend, Shikazo Abe, to find him an apartment. "I want to move out of the president's official residence as soon as I quit," Sogo said, "and I don't want anything said at this time."

When Abe went to a friend who had apartments to rent, he was teased about seeking a place for his mistress. Abe smiled and rented a one-room apartment, but Sogo told him he needed a larger place because he expected many visitors. Abe went back to the landlord and asked for a two-room unit. "I need more space for my beautiful mistress," he said, "and her name is Shinji Sogo."

"Oh," said the landlord, "I have been reading about him. It will be a great honor to have him as a tenant."

While Sogo was left hanging in the breeze, the politicians were conferring quietly to find his successor. The man exerting the most influence in the search was Taizo Ishizaka, the forceful chairman of Keidanren, the Federation of Economic Organizations made up of more than 1,000 of Japan's largest corporations. His candidate was Reisuke Ishida, a member of the National Railways Advisory Council who had opposed *Shinkansen* from the beginning and was outspokenly critical of Sogo's budget overruns. The story circulating at the time was that Ishida spent an evening listening to a tape of Mozart's *Requiem* before agreeing to accept Ishizaka's offer of nomination.

Meanwhile, Sogo prepared for his departure with quiet dignity. On May 17, two days before his last official day, he went to make his farewells to the minister of transportation and held a press conference afterward. The first question was about his health.

"I am fine," Sogo responded, "but I have been suffering from an itchy skin and sometimes cannot sleep. I also have allergies. The University Hospital regards my body as an excellent subject for medical research."

Another reporter asked how he felt about leaving JNR. Sogo responded with a haiku he had composed, a 17-syllable poem in which feeling and imagination are projected to create a mental rather than specific picture. In rough translation: "Spring thunder/ roaring along/ 20,000 railroad lines."

Asked about his most memorable experience, Sogo did not hesitate. "It was the recent Mikawashima Station disaster," he said. "I inspected the accident site and visited the family of each victim. In one home an old woman knelt in front of an altar praying for her son who had been killed in the crash. I wept with her. For a whole month after that, I wept whenever I thought of her."

Finally a reporter, violating peculiarly Japanese protocol, screwed up the courage to ask about the *Shinkansen* budget. Sogo replied: "I am totally responsible for the ¥80 billion overrun, and I apologize. I tried to create a superb railway at minimal expense, but I did not succeed. National Railways will face extreme financial difficulties for the immediate future. Something has to be done. One obvious way to reduce the deficit is to create higher profits. That can be accomplished. The Tokaido *Shinkansen* will be a profitable operation."

Someone asked Sogo what he thought of his apparent

successor, Reisuke Ishida. Sogo replied courteously: "Mr. Ishida is a veteran businessman, and he knows about business. I am sure he will achieve what I could not."

Ishida was not so gracious. It was widely reported that when Sogo turned over the president's office to him, Ishida remarked: "You are leaving us with a spoiled baby (a reference to the *Shinkansen*). I don't know how much we will have to suffer before we overcome its problems."

Despite all the successful tests, Ishida still was unconvinced about *Shinkansen*'s safety. Shortly after he took over, three members of the royal family—Princess Chichibu, Prince Takamatsu, and Prince Mikasa—were scheduled to take a demonstration ride. While they waited for royalty to board, Ishida said to Shima: "I hate the *Shinkansen*. Inheriting such a dangerous thing, I am in real trouble. It is still being tested, and these very important people are going to ride it. What will happen if they are injured?"

Shima could hardly control his anger.

Prince Takamatsu, who had been on a test run earlier with Sogo and Shima, overheard Ishida and said, "You needn't be worried. All the experts are confident the train is safe. Shall I have the newspaper photographer take my picture now so they can publish it as the last photo of Prince Takamatsu?" Laughter broke the tension.

At the end of May, some low-level National Railways employees organized a reception for Sogo at the Tokyo Station Hotel. The hall's capacity was 250, but more than 500 jammed the room. When Sogo arrived, firecrackers were set off and a band played. "Thank you for your leadership, Sogo-san," the crowd shouted. "Well done! Good luck! Live long!"

In his response, Sogo said: "You wish me a long life, and I thank you. I want you to know I intend to live 200 years. But my life was shortened by 20 years by grief over the Mikawashima

Station tragedy. So I promise you, I intend to live until I am 180 years old." That set off another round of cheers.

Soon after Sogo left the presidency, Shima and other leading members of his team resigned. Their work was nearly done and for them, an era had ended.

In the months after his retirement, Sogo traveled to various parts of the network to bid workers farewell and thank them for the years they had served the railways. Everywhere he was hailed as the beloved leader. One day he attended the unveiling of a monument to the memory of 210 workmen who had lost their lives building *Shinkansen*. The inscription carved into the stone was in Sogo's distinctive handwriting.

Elaborate festivities marked the opening of *Shinkansen* service. The official dedication was on September 30, 1964, when for the last time a test run was made from Tokyo to Osaka. Sogo was invited to the ceremonies before the test run but assigned to a seat for "others" in a remote area and was not recognized. Many Very Important Persons rode the train to Osaka, where there was another reception, but Sogo was not among them. The next day, October 1, there were two celebrations. The first was at 6 a.m. when the symbolic ribbon was cut and the first official trip began. Sogo was not invited. At 10 a.m., when the opening ceremony was held at the JNR headquarters in Tokyo in the presence of Emperor Hirohito and Empress Nagako, Sogo sat unnoticed off in a corner.

"By then," says his youngest son Shinsaku, "I don't think it really mattered to Shinji Sogo that he was not treated as a VIP. The inner sense of accomplishment was more important to him than a moment of glory at the Emperor's side."

Where was Shima? Friends said he waited to see his baby's first run from the roof of his apartment house. His expression did not change, but his eyes were misty as he watched the beautiful train pick up speed and vanish into the distance.

If others did not notice the slights, the Imperial Household Agency seemed to be aware of it. Customarily, government ministries are asked to submit nominees each year for recognition by the Emperor. Sogo was asked by his successor, Reisuke Ishida, if he would agree to be nominated. Sogo asked whether Shima also would be nominated. Ishida promised that Shima would be nominated the following year. Only then did Sogo agree to have his name submitted.

A year after the ribbon-cutting, Sogo was decorated by Emperor Hirohito with the Grand Cordon of the Order of the Sacred Treasure, an award reserved for only the most distinguished citizens for extraordinary accomplishment and service to the nation. He was proud of the decoration, but also proud that isolated little Saijo City, where he had served as the unpaid, forward-looking mayor, named him as its first and only honorary citizen and erected his bust in a public park.

The reasons Sogo has not received the recognition he deserved in Japan for getting *Shinkansen* built are not clearly understood. One suggestion is that many JNR bureaucrats, who never became comfortable with Sogo's leadership, lost no opportunity to criticize him in front of his successor, Reisuke Ishida, in an effort to curry the boss's favor. Ishida was president of National Railways when the Bullet Train finally began operations and has received extensive press credit as the major contributor to the progress of Japan's railroad industry. Some years ago *Bungei Shunju*, the leading serious magazine, published the names of 100 "Builders of Japan." Ishida was on the list as a railroad builder. Sogo was not mentioned.

有法子

CHAPTER 23

SILENT THUNDER

Shinji Sogo was 80 years old when the Bullet Trains began their swift journeys in 1964, and beginning to feel the infirmities of age. He had cataract operations on both eyes in 1968. The surgery was not entirely successful. His hearing began to fail. Mostly, he lived quietly in his apartment attended by his private secretary and nurse, Shigeko Takagi. But his mind remained sharp, and he kept up with national and international affairs, reading with the aid of strong lenses, enjoying good conversation with old friends.

In March of 1978 he fell and broke a leg. After that he was confined to a wheelchair. Three years later he was stricken with a high fever and never fully recovered. He died on October 3, 1981, after six months of hospitalization. Pneumonia, compounded by old age, was the cause of death. He had lived 97 years and 7 months through some of his country's most turbulent years. Sogo was aware that in death he was as likely to be surrounded by controversy as he was through much of his life, and carefully scripted the three funerals that he would be accorded.

There was to be a simple, private funeral attended by family and close friends. His ashes were to be interred with those of his wife, Kiku, at the Risho-ji Temple in Suginami Ward, Tokyo.

Following that would be an official public funeral at Aoyama Memorial Hall. Sogo left word that he did not wish to have flowers, but if flowers were sent nonetheless, they should be displayed without identifying the donor. And because important donors, some of whom may not have been friends, would want to have their flowers placed where they would attract the greatest attention, he specified that no preference should be given to anyone. And finally, he asked for a simple memorial service near his birthplace on Shikoku.

It would have been nice to think that, for a moment, every Bullet Train in Japan would slide to a stop in his memory. But Old Man Thunder would have frowned on that kind of display as a pretentious intrusion on National Railways' timetables. The thunder was stilled, but not the spirit behind it.

有法子

EPILOGUE

While *Shinkansen*'s first Tokyo-Osaka runs were scheduled
for four hours, soon they were making the 320-mile trip in three
hours—at an average speed of 128 miles per hour. In the first
three decades of operation, *Shinkansen* trains carried more than
2.8 billion passengers, saving them billions of hours of travel
time, without a single fatality.

Today many of *Shinkansen*'s cars are double-deckers that
provide more seating as well as a better view of the fleeting
countryside. Every few minutes during rush hours, almost as
frequently as the subways under Tokyo and Osaka, *Shinkansen*
trains leave the two cities. A recent *Shinkansen* timetable gives

travelers a choice of more than 140 trains daily each way between Tokyo and Osaka—18 Nozomi Superexpress trains, about 100 Hikari express trains, and 24 Kodama local trains. Some Japanese commute 100 miles or more each day by Bullet Train to jobs in Tokyo from homes in less crowded towns. Advanced models of *Shinkansen* trains race between Tokyo and more remote parts of Honshu Island, through an undersea tunnel, to the metropolis of Hakata on Kyushu Island in the southwest and Morioka in the far northeast. *Shinkansen*'s steel network, fed by the capillaries of local lines, has revolutionized life in Japan in a way that not even Shinji Sogo could have envisioned. No part of the nation, except distant isles, can now be considered remote.

In 1970 Masaru Ibuka, a cofounder of the vast Sony electronics company that helped revolutionize the way the world hears music and sees pictures in color on glass tubes, spoke at an *Asahi Shimbun* seminar. He recalled his early experiences in designing tape recorders and transistor radios, and then he switched to the subject of *Shinkansen*.

"I am about to go to the United States as a member of a mission of Japanese business executives," he said, "and we will visit NASA, the American space agency. I was looking for a big Japanese project to compare with their Apollo Space Project. I picked *Shinkansen* and wrote a report titled 'The Management of a National Project.' I identified a number of reasons for its success.

"First, the genius of Hideo Shima, the engineer, which was recognized by Shinji Sogo who went to extraordinary lengths to hire him and then was wise enough to give him free rein.

"Second, Sogo's successful lobbying of government and business leaders to support his goal of putting together a new standard-gauge railroad, which he believed, despite public opinion to the contrary, to be best for his country.

"Third, Sogo's audacity in pushing the *Shinkansen* start-up bill through the National Diet, even to the extent of presenting a draft budget of ¥190 billion when he was aware the final cost would be closer to ¥300 billion.

"Fourth, building public support by disseminating information through the media and organizing seminars.

"Fifth, consensus-building through the process of *nema-washi* at every critical level of the project.

"Sixth, success in winning the financial support of the World Bank, which meant not only necessary funds, but equally important, credibility.

"I call these efforts 'persuasion technology.' While Shima was working in the laboratory, Sogo was spending most of his time and energy persuading people to support him. The dedication of these two men shows that any worthwhile project, in business or in government, is possible if we believe in it strongly enough and work hard enough. *Shinkansen* did not develop any notable technological innovations, but by harnessing and utilizing what was known, it revived what was regarded internationally as a declining industry.

"When the huge and costly *Shinkansen* project was first announced, I, like the majority of Japanese, believed the money should be spent on building automobile expressways instead of a railroad. We know now that the *Shinkansen* project was the result of the dedication of people who believed in the value of standard-gauge railroads. We tend to think that it is most important to create a good organization to achieve good results, and that if the organization is good, good results will be easily achieved. In *Shinkansen*, an organization had nothing to do with its success. This great result was achieved solely because of the long-cherished belief and determination of one man, whose name is Shinji Sogo."

A noble tribute indeed. But the real memorial to Shinji

Sogo is not to be found in words or monuments, but in the safe, reliable, swift-moving, pulsating *Shinkansen* transportation system that unites his nation as nothing else can.

GLOSSARY AND TERMS

aka gami—draft notice; *aka* means "red"
Bushido—a feudal-military code of chivalry valuing honor above life
furoshiki—wrapping cloth
fuurin—wind chimes which were visible but accomplished nothing
Gokoku-ki—flag to defend the fatherland; flag of Ichiko School
hotto shita—to feel relieved
Kaminari Oyaji—Old Man Thunder
koku—one koku is a fraction less than 10 cubic feet
Kumako—bear cub; Shinji Sogo's nickname at Ichiko School
kyo—cooperation
Kyosan-to—Communist party
Kyoto Imperial University—became Kyoto University after World War II
nemawashi—carefully digging around a tree to prepare it for transplanting
sen—monetary unit; 100th part of a yen
Shinkansen—New Trunk Line; a high-speed passenger railroad system
shoji—light screen made with wood frame and paper covering, used as a sliding
    panel between interior or exterior spaces
sosai—a president or a governor
sumi ink—a black ink made from a mixture of plant soot and glue solidified
    into sticks or cakes
Tokyo Imperial University—became Tokyo University after World War II
tsubo—a unit to measure property (=35.6 sq. ft.)
yen—monetary unit equivalent to 100 *sen*
youchi-asagake—a day-and-night raid; a term to describe the press barging in on
    politicians or celebrities for interviews regardless of
    the time of day
yukata robe—informal summer kimono

Chinese Names and Locations

Wade-Giles/Postal Atlas of China (Pre-1950)	Pinyin (After 1950)
Antung	Andong
Canton	Guangzhou
Chang Jiang	Yangtze River
Chang Tso-lin	Zhang Zuolin
Dairen	Dalian
Chefoo	Yantai
Hsinking	Changchun
Mount Manpo	Wanpaoshan
Mukden	Shenyang
Nanking	Nanjing
Peking	Beijing
Tientsin	Tianjin

INDEX